Web Site Privacy with P3P®

Web Site Privacy with P3P®

Helena Lindskog
Stefan Lindskog

WILEY
Wiley Publishing, Inc.

Publisher: Robert Ipsen
Editor: Carol A. Long
Developmental Editor: Adaobi Obi Tulton
Editorial Manager: Kathryn Malm
Managing Editor: Pamela M. Hanley
Text Design & Composition: Wiley Composition Services

This book is printed on acid-free paper. ♾

Published simultaneously in Canada

Library of Congress Cataloging-in-Publication Data:

Lindskog, Helena, 1966-
Web site privacy with P3P / Helena Lindskog, Stefan Lindskog.
p. cm.
ISBN 0-471-21677-1
1. Computer networks—Security measures. 2. World Wide Web—Security measures.
3. Web sites—Security measures. 4. Privacy, Right of. I.
Lindskog, Stefan, 1967- II. Title.
TK5105.59 .L56 2003
005.8—dc21
2002155538

Printed in the United States of America

10 9 8 7 6 5 4 3 2 1

To our wonderful children Caroline, Sofia, David and Johanna

CONTENTS

ACKNOWLEDGMENTS

For very valuable advising and proofreading, we would like to thank: Andreas Ljunggren, Mikael Nilsson, Giles Hogben, Jörgen Sigvardsson, Johan Hjelm, Magnus Johnard, and Fredric Palmgren.

Stephen Kenny

CHAPTER 1

Introduction to Privacy

Privacy in Internet environments is not only about technology and legislation, but also about straightforwardness, in both directions. It is about making sure that sites are up-front with the people using their services, and it is about providing the end user with the choice of whether to share information with the origin server.

This book is about how to use technology in the service of end users.

Privacy Awareness

The struggle for respect for privacy has always been an ongoing battle. In 1890, after the press had published some personal information about the Warren family, Louis Brandeis and Samuel Warren wrote "The Right to Privacy," where they defined privacy as a fundamental right of the individual that should not be tampered with.

Our opinions of and feelings toward privacy vary for a number of factors. The first is our age. Our respect for authorities varies with the time we were born. People born in the 1940s and 1950s appear to have less respect for authorities than do people born in the 1920s and 1930s; those of us born in the 1960s grew up in shock over the controversial behavior of grown-ups.

The rights of "normal" individuals are one thing—what about the rights of those not like us? Lobotomy was used until the end of the 1970s in most countries, and sterilization of the mentally challenged is still discussed. However slowly, a common understanding of the rights of people who are different from ourselves in some aspect is developing over the world, and the younger we are, the more natural this understanding is to us.

Another interesting difference is how the new generation, which never knew a world without email and SMS[1], views privacy. Our two daughters would never dream of chatting using their own names. They each have a personal email address that uses the family domain, which they use with their close friends, and one public address, where they have given themselves nicknames like skate_girl_160@hotmail.com. How the concept of pseudonymization got into their minds, we do not know, but for some reason we think the next generation will claim their right to privacy with a lot more enthusiasm than the rest of us.

A second factor that makes us different from each other is our cultural background and nationality. In Sweden, we have a concept of openness that influences the way we all think. We have not participated in a war since the beginning of the nineteenth century, so military supervision has not been a routine part of our lives. According to Swedish law, the salary of any citizen who has a job in the public sector, such as a schoolteacher, is public. The salaries are printed in a book that anyone can buy. On the other hand, due to the lack of military supervision, there is little chance that privacy laws are broken for the sake of public safety. In countries that have been exposed to severe threats, like Germany during the 1950s to 1970s and the United States in 2001, the understanding that police and military authorities may have to bend the rights of individuals to stop real danger is much greater.

In some countries there is distrust of those same authorities. Those who live in countries that have suppressed their people, or at least some groups of their people, have a greater suspicion of their government's data collection activities. For instance, many Germans may have experienced first-hand crimes committed by the Nazi as well as the East German regimes.

Our cultural background, our experiences, and those of our parents and grandparents thus affect our views of privacy. What about religion and gender? Do Christian women have a different view of privacy than

[1] Short Message Service - text messages received to your mobile device.

Muslim men? Well, of course. Our social status is also a factor. Even if we find two Finnish women, aged 43, both of whom had fathers who fought in World War II, are Protestants, and have the same income, they may well feel very different from each other.

This brings us to one other basic definition of privacy, made by Alan Westin in 1967:

> *Privacy is the claim of individuals, groups, and institutions to determine for themselves how, when, and to what extent information about them is communicated to others.*

In other words, privacy is about self-determination. As individuals, we need to decide for ourselves what we want. We do not want to be treated as a group of tourists pushed around Versailles on the assumption that we all wish to see the bed of Louis XIV instead of having a closer look at the paintings of Marie Antoinette.

We may have very good reasons for wanting privacy. We may be trying to avoid divorce attorneys or the Mafia. We may have no more specific reasons than simply to exercise our right to be left alone. Note that this would not be a chapter about privacy if this factor was not mentioned: We may also be criminals trying to hide illegal deeds. Regardless of whether this illegal deed is distribution of copyrighted material, burglary, or terrorism, the fact remains: Providing individuals with rights, such as freedom of speech, the right to an attorney, or the right to privacy, might be advantageous to a criminal. A phone can be used for criminal purposes. So can a car, a computer, and the Internet.

We are not going to dwell on the issue of privacy versus crime for long because many scientific papers have been written on the subject, but there are two things we would like you to bear in mind. The first is that if we really want to send a message from, say, Australia to Seattle using the Internet, without anybody noticing, there are about 50 ways to do it, and none of them involves the use of P3P. The second is that our feelings about privacy may well depend on all the factors we previously stated.

Even if we, as individuals, decide that we do not think this privacy stuff is very interesting, and even if we do not care if people want to collect our IP numbers, there is still the business perspective. Valued customers who visit our business Web sites care about privacy, and will abandon our sites if we do not show that we care as well. We should respect the rights of individuals to determine for themselves whether they want private information communicated to others. If you want your customer's respect, you should convey the following message to your customer:

"I, your local friendly service provider, respect your right to self-determination."

The Right to Be Left Alone

Have you ever received a spam email? Our first experience with it was a few years ago when our then nine-year-old daughter's mailbox was filled with ads for sex sites. We were completely outraged. We tried to put a stop to it any way we could, including contacting the ISP and, silly enough, sending "unsubscribe" messages to those sending the email. We know better now, of course. Sending an unsubscribe message has the opposite effect because it proves to the originator of the offending message that there is someone receiving it at the other end.

There are three kinds of privacy, all of which have bearing on the use of Internet:

- *Personal privacy against moral offense,* meaning that we should not be exposed to information that offends our moral senses
- *Territorial privacy against trespassing,* meaning that people should not trespass on our property
- *Informational privacy against gossip,* meaning that we decide about data that can be tied to us as individuals

When our daughter received these messages, it was a violation to all three kinds of privacy. First, someone obviously had collected her email address and sold it, implying disrespect for her informational privacy. Second, they sent email messages that she did not want, showing disrespect for her territorial privacy because it is fair to call our inboxes our territory. After all, they are part of our computers. We should decide for ourselves what should end up there. Third, the links that were sent contained offensive content—fortunately she was too young to follow them—and were thus an intrusion to her personal privacy.

When we discuss privacy issues, we should keep these differences in mind. There are ways to handle all three, but in this book, we focus on informational privacy, which is, in most cases, the starting point for most personal and territorial intrusions. Surveys have shown that exposure to unsolicited email and SMS messages is the greatest privacy concern for most people. Thus, this message should also be conveyed to your customers:

"I will not share identifiable information about you with others."

Means for Privacy

In order to create applications for the privacy-aware user, we need to think like that user. With that in mind, it is now time to introduce our users: Hans and Greta. Hans is the careless sort of person who has never given privacy two thoughts. He will freely give out information, without ever considering that it could be used for something else. He will just shake his head at the fourth Viagra spam he got this week and delete it. Greta wants to stay away from the spotlight, and if she thinks that a service will store or process her information for purposes other than what she intended, she will not use it. She would rather walk to the ATM to get cash for groceries than use her credit and bonus cards where she runs the risk of having information about her purchase stored somewhere for the future.

This book is dedicated to Greta. So why do we need Hans? Even though a user like Hans has no interest in maintaining privacy, he must still have access to all the services he wishes. When we design sites for the privacy-aware user, like Greta, we must consider the ease of use for users like Hans as well, in addition to the legislation of the country where that lives.

Greta wants to go to a Web site that sells the particular book she wants to purchase. She does not want anyone to know what she reads or buys. Let's take a look at her options.

There are four kinds of privacy-enhancing technologies (PETs) defined by the Common Criteria[2] group:

1. Anonymization
2. Pseudonymization
3. Unlinkability
4. Unobservability

[2] The Common Criteria represents the outcome of a series of efforts to develop criteria for evaluation of IT security that are broadly useful within the international community. See http://www.commoncriteria.org/.

Anonymization

The Common Criteria (CC) definition of anonymity is as follows:

> *Anonymity requires that other users or subjects are unable to determine the identity of a user bound to a subject or operation.*

No identifiable information reaches the origin server.

Figure 1.1 Anonymity.

Anonymization, as illustrated in Figure 1.1, implies that the destination will not know who Greta is at all. If Greta uses a technology of this kind, she will be completely anonymous to the origin server.

What is interesting to note, though, is that even though people want anonymity, few are willing to pay for it. In 1998, a Canadian company called ZeroKnowledge did an implementation of the Chaum white papers, which introduced a technology called mix nets that allows anonymous transmissions to take place. It called the service the Freedom Network. In October 2001, the network was closed down—mainly for financial reasons.

The end user will or might have to pay for anonymity in several ways:

- The cost that the company will charge Greta to use the service
- The cost of overhead when it comes to deciding which service to use and why it is good—such as whether to trust the ISP's services or to select a third party
- The cost of round-trip times—that is, the number of extra seconds that Greta will have to wait to get to the requested URL

There is another not-so-irrelevant problem in the particular case of Greta wanting to buy books. She can be anonymous when surfing around looking for them, but how will she pay for them without having her identity revealed? Well, it is possible. There are technologies for digital cash transmissions that are based on the same ideas as cash cards, but they have three drawbacks. One is that they are complex and rarely used. Another is that they are not secure—that is, money can be lost, just as you can lose money by misplacing your wallet, which means that the concept should be used only for smaller amounts. The main reason, though, is that banks may use these transactions to preserve data about which user issued which check. All this means the following:

- A lot of overhead
- Difficulty and uncertainty when it comes to getting back lost money
- A willingness to trust the bank with the customer's privacy

Let's suppose that Greta wants anonymity so badly that she will still take the overhead of using an anonymous routing protocol to reach the origin server and will use digital cash for the payment. How is the vendor supposed to ship the goods to her if she does not want to give away her identity?

Pseudonymity

The CC definition says the following:

> *Pseudonymity requires that a set of users and/or subjects are unable to determine the identity of a user bound to a subject or operation, but that this user is still accountable for its actions.*

The general idea of pseudonymization is that you use an identity that cannot be tied to you as a person—that is, an alias or a nickname. It could also be a serial number. Pseudonyms are used, for example, when providing location data from a telecom operator to a service provider; see Appendix D. There are several ways of doing this, but in general the location is passed on with a number that will identify the user throughout the session.

Thus, the pseudonym is a recurring ID that is indirectly tied to the user. The matter of accountability is relevant according to the CC definition;

the pseudonym is reversible, if it is really necessary for reasons of crime or nonrepudiation. This obviously does not include the case where the user pseudonymizes herself (Figure 1.2). Cases can fall outside the scope of the CC definition, and we would prefer lifting the issue of accountability out of the definition.

Pseudonymization can also take place at the receiving side. Pseudonymizing databases to be able to store data longer than allowed by law is a common method, used when building statistical databases, for example.

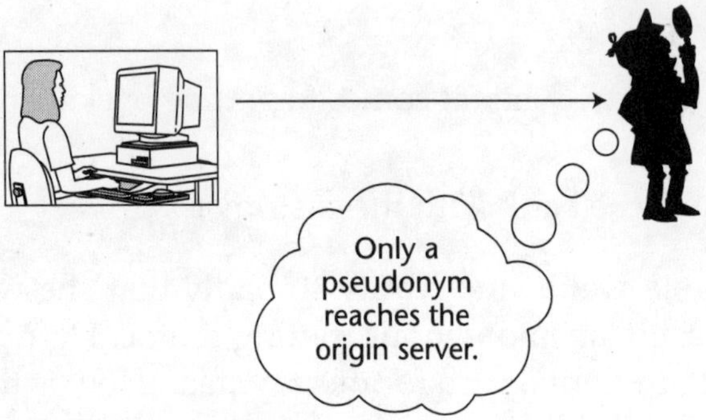
Only a
pseudonym
reaches the
origin server.

Figure 1.2 Pseudonymity.

The pseudonymity concept is what teenagers use when they use weird Hotmail addresses to communicate with people they do not know. Pseudonymity also occurs when you create an account with your favorite Internet chess club, calling yourself "Bobby Fischer II" or when you play Quake as "The Mega Wizard." It is often used in statistical databases. Origin servers that want to keep data for statistical purposes can pseudonymize this data before storing it.

Unlinkability

The third category defined by the CC says the following:

Unlinkability requires that users and/or subjects are unable to determine whether the same user caused certain specific operations in the system.

Figure 1.3 Unlinkability.

In this particular case, the user is part of a group that has access to the service, but no one can determine which one in the group actually performed the specific operation. You can see that the group that Greta is part of sent the request to the server, but not that she was the one who did it. To benefit from this, Greta would need to join a network of users that collectively use a privacy protocol that implies that no one can determine from which particular person in the network the action took place.

Unobservability

Finally, the last category of privacy-enhancing technologies is unobservability. The CC definition says the following:

> *Unobservability requires that users and/or subjects cannot determine whether an operation is being performed.*

This is about getting the message through without anybody noticing that a message was even transmitted. A common method is steganography, where a message is hidden inside something else. This could be a picture, downloaded from the Web, an audio file, or even a simple text message. If you were the kind of kid who liked playing detective or spy, you have probably tried the last category. You often see this kind of technology used in Hollywood movies, where a character receives an email message with no meaning, then the letters suddenly change places, and a secret message is shown.

Figure 1.4 Unobservability.

Unobservability is about hiding from the rest of the world, not the receiver, which is why it has no bearing on Greta's particular problem.

The Origin Server Perspective

We are still stuck with a problem. Greta wants access to a service. Somewhere there is an origin server that wants to provide her with this service, but neither one can reach the other. The reason why they cannot is simple: lack of trust. If Greta had trusted services on the Internet in the first place, there would not be a problem.

Let's take a look at the bookstore, which we will call werespectyou.com. This is a nice little company that tries hard to meet the needs and wishes of its customers. At this company work two Web designers named Harry and Sally, who have learned in the past few years that personalization is important. Thus, they provide users like Hans with a number of features to improve his experience when he visits their site. They remember the books he has bought and send him email messages in which they state that because he bought a book about monkeys last time he was there, he might be interested in a new, particularly interesting book about gorillas. He has made settings in which he stated that he is interested in sports and music; thus, they can tailor the site when he reaches it to make sure that books concerning these subjects are the first he sees whenever he logs on. They have placed cookies on his client, so that he barely even needs to log on. Any time he wants to buy something from the site, his name and address are automatically filled out for him on the order form. In order to do this, werespectyou.com has stored a lot of data about Hans. This data is also used for statistical purposes so that the company can build customer profiles and make strategic decisions about what books to have in stock in the future.

werespectyou.com also has a system administrator named Karen who has a hard time chasing hackers out of the system. She keeps log files of all the activities, so if Trudy the intruder breaks in or makes an attempt to, Karen will be ready to catch her. This activity takes place in the basement of the company, where the servers are located. When Karen first installed the Web server, she used the standard logging facilities, but as the company has grown, the number of attempted intrusions has grown to several a week, and now she has created several Perl scripts that log everything. Those log files are sometimes cleaned, but some of them remain on DAT tapes in a closet. That way, she knows that she can retrieve those files to track an intruder if she comes back.

In essence, werespectyou.com has the following needs:

- Collect data about the buyer, in order to fulfill the request
- Collect data about all users to create statistical reports
- Keep log files about activities in order to maintain an acceptable level of security
- Profile the user, in order to enhance the user's experience at the Web site

When the Origin Server Meets the Privacy-Aware User

Three extreme categories of people reach werespectyou.com: Hans, Greta, and Trudy the intruder. Karen handles Trudy. Harry and Sally have already created customized applications for Hans. Now it is time to take care of Greta's needs. Before we do that, we need to take a closer look at which one of the previously listed needs of the company is absolutely necessary.

It is necessary to collect data about the buyer in order to fulfill the request, but is it necessary to store this data? Well, it is useful but not necessary. If werespectyou.com wants Greta as a customer, it should consider retaining Greta's data only at the time of the purchase, then erasing it.

Statistics are important; however, there are ways to store data that is anonymized or at least pseudonymized that can fulfill that purpose without losing quality or compromising the user's privacy. Some countries, like Germany, have laws that require that all data collected for statistical purposes be pseudonymized.

The dilemma now is this: How can we balance security and privacy? There are three answers to this. One is reversible pseudonymization—that is, log files can be written, but any personal data that is stored must first be pseudonymized so that it can be retrieved only if it is actively demanded. The other solution is selection. Not everything needs to be logged. We look into this more in a later chapter. The third solution is retention. The log files can safely be deleted after a specific period of time—for example, after two weeks. This is all about balancing Karen's and Greta's needs.

Profiling is a feature that Hans really appreciates. It gives business advantages to the company. We do not want to take this away from the company. In Greta's case, though, profiling is a nuisance. She would feel terribly offended by a "Hello, Greta, we have some new books that might interest you" message. The tricky part is distinguishing Greta from Hans.

Self-determination is one thing, but the question lies in how to communicate with the end user in a way that does not imply a lot of overhead. By the end of this book, we will have fully answered this question. For the time being, let's go back to Greta's particular problem.

If she knew that werespectyou.com would retain her personal data only long enough to perform her purchase, that all data used for statistical purposes would be completely pseudonymized, that Web server log files would be deleted after two weeks, that only one person would have access to them during this time, and that no data would be stored for profiling purposes, she would consider buying her books there. So, how can she know? She can go to the site and read the privacy policy file posted there. Before she learns about the site's policy, though, the site may have already collected a lot of personal information about her. It also takes time to read and understand a policy file. As Greta wanders out to the Internet café on the corner to read the policy file anonymously, she wishes that there was a means for companies to create policy files that ensured that her privacy was completely preserved while reading it and that the policy file would be written in a generic, computer-readable way so that she could make settings on her computer against which the policy file could be matched.

Platform for Privacy Preferences

The Platform for Privacy Preferences Project (P3P) was started about five years ago to define a means to publish Web site policies in a machine-readable way. The project is run by a World Wide Web Consortium (W3C) working group, and it has published a specification that is currently a proposed recommendation. The latest version of the specification can be found at http://www.w3.org/TR/P3P/. We spend several chapters describing P3P in detail, so this is just a short introduction.

In order to perform a P3P agreement, illustrated in Figure 1.5, we must have a P3P-enabled site, where two files are stored:

- A reference file
- A policy file

That's it—no magic. The reference file will tell which policy file applies to which resource—for example, the homepage—and the policy file will state the privacy policy for the whole site or just a specific part of the site.

Greta has a user-agent that can act on her behalf. This user-agent either is built into her browser or is a plug-in to her browser. It can also be a proxy, located somewhere else. In connection with this user-agent, she has stored her preferences, in a format called APPEL, which is also XML based.

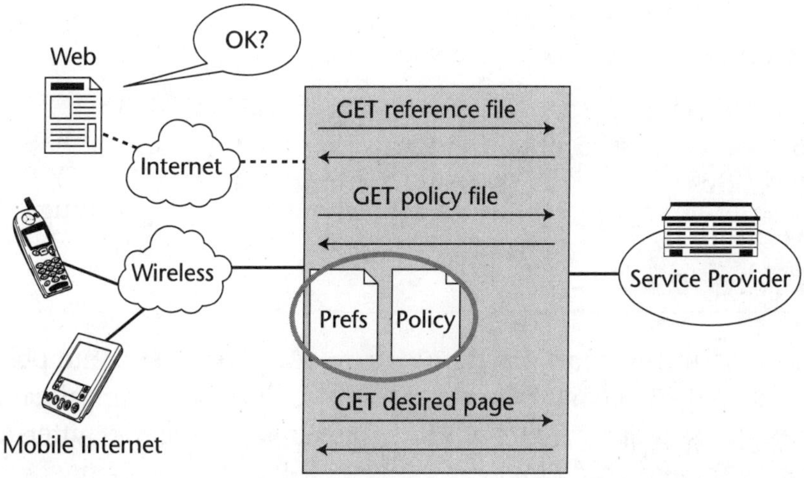

Figure 1.5 A P3P agreement.

The task of the user-agent is to retrieve the correct policy file for the page where she wants to go and to compare its content with Greta's stored preferences. If there is a mismatch, the user-agent will probably ask Greta if she wants to retrieve the site anyway. The agreement takes place in a so-called "safe-zone," where no data is supposed to be sent by the user-agent or stored by the origin server.

Trust

Harry and Sally have created policy files (after reading this book, it took them only about 30 minutes), and Greta has acquired a user-agent that can store her preferences and perform the agreement. There is only one issue left: How does Greta know that werespectyou.com will indeed keep its promises? How can she be sure that Harry and Sally took the time explain to Karen that it is now prohibited to store more data than necessary and for longer than necessary? How can she be sure that they actually implemented all the privacy-aware features that they say they did? Well, she cannot be sure. There is no feature in P3P that makes sure that the origin server does what it states it will do. This is where we have to introduce a new concept called trust. Trust is what you, as a serious company, will gain from your customers when you do what you say you will. Some countries go further. Some people demand that all privacy policies, whether written in P3P or in a natural language, be legally binding, like any other contract. This will, of course, enhance Greta's sense of safety. Therefore, strong privacy legislation is not always a threat to origin servers, but rather a possibility of gaining privacy-aware users as your customers.

In countries where there is no such legislation, you will have to rely on your good name to obtain the trust of your users. The best way to achieve this is never to misuse their confidence.

What's Ahead

Throughout this book, we discuss how Web designers like Harry and Sally manage to change their company's privacy-awareness in order to better fit the requirements of users like Greta and Hans, while keeping trespassers like Trudy away.

We start by looking into Internet security and standard Internet architectures. If you are well aware of these already, you can skip Chapters 2 and 3. We then go through privacy risks on the Internet before we cover privacy-enhancing technologies. We also discuss privacy versus security and different tools to perform the tasks necessary at the origin server without compromising the user's privacy more than necessary.

After this, we start with P3P and how the nice privacy features can be described in a policy file. We go through the tools available and discuss several user scenarios. We then discuss how P3P will be used in the future, and particularly in mobile environments, where there will be so much more data to protect than in traditional Internet environments.

Legislation is an important aspect of privacy, and throughout this book, we discuss how the current legislation will affect tomorrow's services.

It is our hope that this chapter has served as an introduction to both P3P policies and to creating services that respect the user's right to privacy and self-determination.

CHAPTER 2

Internet Security

In this chapter, we define and discuss the concept of computer and network security. We start with some basic terminology and definitions, followed by a discussion of the security threats. We also cover different protection mechanisms in this chapter.

Terminology and Definitions

The traditional definition of computer security is that it consists of three different aspects or dimensions: confidentiality, integrity, and availability, as illustrated in Figure 2.1.

Confidentiality, or secrecy, is defined as the prevention of unauthorized disclosure of information, while *integrity*[1] is the prevention of unauthorized modification of information. *Availability* is the prevention of unauthorized withholding of information or resources. These three attributes are often collectively referred to as the CIA, and we could think of them as the ultimate security goals of a particular system.

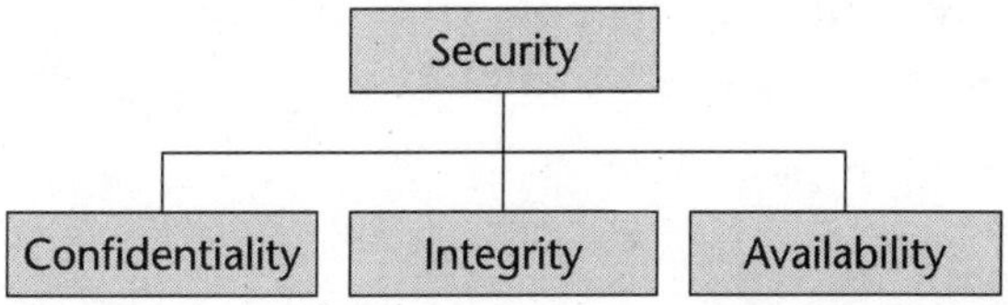

Figure 2.1 Traditional definition of computer security.

[1]Note for completeness that other definitions of the term "integrity" also exist.

Other security goals in addition to the CIA may also be present. *Nonrepudiation* and *message authentication* are two very common examples of additional security goals in a distributed environment. Nonrepudiation requires that neither the sender nor the receiver of a message can reject the transmission. Messsage authentication, on the other hand, ensures that the sender of a message is correctly identified, with an assurance that the identity is not false.

NOTE

Many people erroneously believe that confidentiality and privacy are synonyms. That is not the case because confidentiality does not necessarily have to deal with personal data, which privacy always does. A confidentiality requirement may be due to the fact that highly sensitive corporate data, such as trade secrets, is stored or communicated.

Vulnerabilities and Threats

Vulnerabilities, threats, and risks are three related concepts that we discuss in the following sections. It should, however, be stressed that there is no real consensus on the definition of the terms.

Vulnerabilities

All computer systems and application programs often contain several vulnerabilities, which can be used—or rather misused—by an evil user or a malicious program. Almost daily, we can read in the newspapers that systems have been attacked, and the number of attacks seems to grow from day to day. Some of the reasons include the following:

- More and more computer systems are being connected to the Internet, which implies that many more people around the globe have the opportunity to break into the connected systems.
- Ready-made, so-called *exploit scripts* are available on the Internet. These can easily be downloaded from the Internet, then installed and used to attack a system. This implies that today's attacker does not need a deep technical knowledge about the system or application to attack.

- Knowledge about vulnerabilities in systems and applications is very quickly spread to both system administrators and the potential attackers. A system owner can use that information to patch or fix the system, while a perpetrator may use the same information to break in to systems.
- The size and complexity of software are steadily increasing, and large and complex software tends to have many more vulnerabilities than those applications that are small and simple.

System vulnerabilities are introduced in systems during all phases of their life cycles. Hence, vulnerabilities are introduced in the very early specification phases of a system. Vulnerabilities are also introduced during installation or configuration. The reason could simply be that the responsible system administrator does not have enough knowledge of that particular system. Another reason could be that the installation program is vulnerable. Furthermore, end users are yet another source of vulnerabilities.

One possible way to secure a system is by adding new protection mechanisms to it. Virus scanners, firewalls, and intrusion detection systems (IDSs) are all examples of modern and popular security mechanisms that could be introduced in a system to enhance its security. By adding new components to a system, the system becomes larger and the complexity increases. Unfortunately, by adding new protection mechanisms, new vulnerabilities may also be introduced. This means that such mechanisms should be introduced only when necessary and when one can be sure that the result will be a system with increased security.

The other way to secure a system is by eliminating all its vulnerabilities. This is, however, impossible because we can never find all the vulnerabilities of a complex software system. Still, we can try to eliminate all known ones as quickly as possible. Vendors often announce information on newly discovered vulnerabilities. In addition to the vendors, the Computer Emergency Response Team (CERT) at Carnegie Mellon University and other Internet sites offer information about vulnerabilities, incidents, and recommendations on how to eliminate vulnerabilities. Further information about the CERT Coordination Center (CERT/CC) can be found at http://www.cert.org. Sites announcing system vulnerabilities should be checked regularly, and newly discovered flaws should be fixed as quickly as possible.

A combination of the two methods—adding new protection mechanisms and continuously eliminating newly discovered vulnerabilities—is the best way to protect a system against attacks. We should never mistakenly believe that a system is or can be 100 percent secure.

Threats

Threats can be divided into two main categories:

- Insider threats
- Outsider threats

The insider threat occurs when someone related to an organization or company misuses his or her privileges. An insider typically has an account or, at least, access to the system that is attacked. For example, a former employee might still have access to the computer system via a dial-up connection, and the account might still be active. If the person had been fired, he or she might want to get back at the former employer.

The other category is the outsider threat, which is a threat from someone not directly related to the organization or company. An outsider could indeed be any person on the Internet.

Many people claim that the insider threat is a much bigger problem than the outsider threat. Unfortunately, modern protection mechanisms, such as firewalls and IDSs, are mainly intended (and designed) to protect against an evil outsider. This is a somewhat strange situation.

Why are people so much more concerned about external threats than internal ones? We believe that this is due to a historic misunderstanding. A fortress-like defense, where the idea is to separate the good guys on the inside from the bad guys on the outside, has failed so many times in the past. What occurred in Troy is just one historical example. Furthermore, we can never be sure (and should therefore not assume) that all people on the inside of the fortress are indeed good guys. People seem to have forgotten that because, even today, most people within the computer and network security society still believe that a good way (and, in many cases, the only way) to build a defense is based on the old fortress mentality. What is actually needed is a completely new and fresh security paradigm.

Security Policy

Every modern organization should explicitly define a so-called security policy. This policy should indicate the goals of a computer security effort and the willingness to work toward those goals. A security policy should answer the following three questions:

1. Who should be allowed access to the system?
2. Which resources should be accessible in the system?
3. How should access be controlled or regulated?

In essence, a policy should specify the organization's security goals and where the responsibility for security lies. A person should be appointed to the role of security officer within the organization. This person is ultimately responsible for the work with security. This person should be one who has a certain power in the organization—for example, the vice president. The policy should include some kind of statement declaring financial as well as resource support.

Note that the security policy defines what is allowed and what is not. This information is important when dealing with an attack conducted from either side. Without such a document it is an impossible task to judge whether an attack has been performed. This high-level specification of an organization's security goals is used as the base when working with security. When setting up the filtering rules in a firewall, for example, the intention is that they reflect the overall security policy specified for the whole organization.

Protection Mechanisms

Protection mechanisms are the means to enforce the security goals, which should be specified in a security policy. Some protection mechanisms are shipped with the operating system (OS); others are not. We use the term "security extension" to denote a protection mechanism that was not shipped with the operating system and therefore is not an integral part of the operating system. Firewalls, IDSs, and antivirus software are all examples of security extensions.

The following eight common protection mechanisms are discussed further in this chapter. We emphasize both typical OS mechanisms and security extensions. The highlighted mechanisms are as follows:

- Authentication systems
- Access control
- Cryptographic systems
- Auditing
- Firewalls
- IDSs
- Anti-malware software
- Vulnerability scanners

Authentication Systems

Before a user is allowed access to resources, he or she has to log in to the system. The most common way to do that is by entering a username and a password. A password is meant to show proof that you are the person you claim to be. The password should therefore be a secret word between the user and the system. The process of proofing the identity is referred to as *user authentication*.

A password-based authentication system is based on a secret shared between the user and the system. There are, however, other methods that are based on something you have—for example, a smart card—or something you are—for example, fingerprints.

Access Control

After authentication, some resources in the system will be available and can be accessed. Access to resources in a computer system must be protected. When a user, or a program acting on behalf of a user, tries to access a resource, the (operating) system verifies whether he or she is allowed to do so, using an access control mechanism. Access to the resource is granted only if there is positive verification.

In general, two different access control approaches are used:

- Discretionary Access Control (DAC)
- Mandatory Access Control (MAC)

Most commercial systems are based on DAC. It indicates that the resource owner specifies who may access and who may not access the resource. In MAC, on the other hand, a security officer decides who is allowed and who is disallowed access to a particular resource.

Access control can be implemented in a number of different ways. In traditional UNIX, access control groups are used, while Windows NT and many other OSs use access control lists (ACLs).

Cryptographic Systems

Cryptography is the basis of many privacy-enhancing technologies and security mechanisms. The basic idea is that there is a message that needs to be transmitted or stored in a place where it may be exposed to other people that may want to read it or change it without anyone's noticing. You decide to encrypt the message so that only you and the receiver will understand it, whether you and the receiver are actual persons or computer systems.

Risks that can be eliminated with encryption are as follows:

- Someone will read and understand secret information.
- Someone will be able to alter information.
- Someone claims to be someone else.
- Someone denies having been involved in something.

These four risks are actually very different. In most cases, you do not need to handle all of them.

Usage of Cryptographic Systems

Consider a transmission of data between two parties, Alice and Greta.

- Alice does not want anyone to read the message.
- Greta wants to know that Alice is the actual sender of the message.

You are to sign something, and the receiver wants to know for sure that it was you who signed it.

- It does not matter if anyone can read the content.
- It is important that no one else can pretend to be you.

Thus, we have two uses for encryption: signing and secrecy.

The basis in encryption is the key. In principal, there are two different types of encryption systems:

- Symmetric systems
- Asymmetric systems

In a symmetric system, a sender and a receiver have a shared key. This key is used for both encryption and decryption. This type of system is sometimes also referred to as a shared key system. In an asymmetric system, on the other hand, two different types of keys are used—a public key and a private key. The public key is used to encrypt a message, while the private key is used for decryption. Hence, a private key is never disclosed to another party. It can be stored in the computer, in a personal device such as a mobile phone, or on a key card, for example. The idea is that a private key has a public key connected to it that can be sent to anyone. They are then called a pair of keys.

What is encrypted with a public key is decrypted with a private key, and vice versa. This concept can be used both for secrecy and signing. In both cases we will have to ensure the identity of the other party—that is, the fact that the public key does belong to the other party and not someone else—before starting the process.

Public Keys for Signing

You can sign what you want to send with your private key, and the receiver can verify it through decryption with the public key. This way you can identify the receiver. If the point of the signature is to prove your identity, only a small piece of text needs to be signed. If the purpose is to sign a big document, you usually calculate a so-called hash sum, which could be thought of as a cryptographic checksum, which makes it impossible (or at least difficult) to alter the document without the signed hash being wrong.

Public Keys for Secrecy

In order to transmit something that is to be kept a secret from everybody else, you could possibly encrypt it with the public key of the receiver, which will ensure that only the receiver, who holds the private key, will be able to read it. This kind of encryption is time-consuming, which is normally why the standard encryption process is to agree on a shared secret—that is, a string that will be used to encrypt the message, using public key encryption.

RSA, named after its creators, Rivest, Shamir, Adelman, is a frequently used encryption method that uses public and private key pairs. It is considered very secure if the key length is long enough, but it requires a lot of expensive computations by the processor. Secure Socket Layer (SSL) is a transmission protocol for confidentiality, often based on RSA for exchange of shared secret keys, also called session keys. Most often, the HTTP Secure method (HTTPS) uses SSL. Another method is Transmission Layer Security (TLS), and Wireless TLS (WTLS) used in Wireless Application Protocol (WAP) version 1 transmission.

Certificates

A certificate is a standardized record that contains the user ID of a user or entity, the public key, and other fields. The use of certificates for authentication and access control has become widespread during the last few years. Two types of signatures could be distinguished:

- Identity signatures
- Authorization signatures

An identity signature is a proof of identity, while an authorization signature is used for granting access rights.

Digital Signatures

Digital signatures are essentially used for signing documents. Digital signatures could be used to ensure integrity and/or authenticity of a document; see the previous section on public keys for signing.

PKI (Public Key Infrastructure)

PKI is both a method for exchanging public keys and an infrastructure based on the idea of having certificates containing information signed by a certificate authority, which in turn has certificates signed by a certificate authority higher up, and so on. Two different certificate standards are typically used on the Internet:

- X.509, which is a recommendation originally proposed by the Comité Consultatif International de Télégraphique et Téléphonique (CCITT)
- The Simple Public Key Infrastructure (SPKI), which is a proposal by the Internet Engineering Task Force (IETF)

PKI can be used in combination with SSL or TLS to first ensure that the receiver is who he or she claims to be before using the same key for shared secret agreement.

PKI can also be used for signing transactions, like Internet purchases, and documents.

Nonrepudiation means that you cannot deny having done something. Using digital signatures, and PKI in particular, the signing party can be tied to his or her action.

Auditing

The process of monitoring the activity in a system is known as auditing (or logging). Typically, information about activities in the system is stored in special log files on a disk, a tape, or some other type of secondary storage. The purpose of auditing is twofold:

- To verify that the protection mechanisms actually work as intended
- To keep track of what is happening and what has already happened in the system

Auditing is often a built-in mechanism in OSs. In addition, auditing can be done on the application level. Many Internet services, such as HTTP servers, FTP servers, and Telnet servers, perform their own logging. Firewalls, which are described in the following section, are yet another example of a component where logging often is performed.

Firewalls

A firewall is a typical border control mechanism or perimeter defense. The purpose of a firewall is to block traffic from the outside, but it could also be used to block traffic from the inside. There are basically two different types of firewalls: packet filters and proxies.

A packet filter is, in principle, a router with the ability to filter or block traffic to and from a network. Packets to a specific service can also be blocked. IP packets to a computer on an internal network with certain options turned on or off could also be screened. Essentially, information on the TCP/IP level is used to decide whether to allow or disallow a particular type of traffic.

Proxies, on the other hand, act as mediators for traffic passing through them. Two different types of proxies can be distinguished: circuit-level proxies and application-level proxies. The former has many similarities with a packet filter because they base their decisions on the same low-level information—that is, the TCP/IP level—and they are both general devices. The main difference between a circuit-level proxy and a packet filter is that packets sent in a proxy system seem to terminate in the proxy, while packets sent in a packet filtering system keep all their original addresses.

Finally, an application-level proxy is capable of making decisions based on the content of the traffic that passes through it. This implies that an application-level proxy has to be aware of the application-level protocol and is therefore very specialized. A separate proxy is, for example, needed for each application—that is, one for FTP, another one for HTTP, and yet another for Telnet.

Intrusion Detection Systems

The main purpose of an Intrusion Detection System (IDS) is to automatically identify whether an intrusion has occurred or is occurring. Hence, IDSs are essentially burglar alarms for computer systems. An IDS analyzes system data from many different sources, such as OS logs, application logs, and network traffic information.

A database of acceptable and unacceptable behavior is also usually developed and used by the IDS to make decisions. This database may consist of user profiles or patterns of known attacks and is generally referred to as the detection policy.

Anti-Malware Software

Viruses, worms, and Trojan horses are all examples of malicious software, or *malware* for short. Special so-called anti-malware tools are used to detect them and cure an infected system. This type of tool acts as an internal defense mechanism.

The most common type of anti-malware software is (virus) scanners. These tools often consist of two different but related parts: a scanner (or verifier) and a disinfector. The task of the former is to look for malware signatures after they have already entered the system, while the disinfector is used to remove malware from an infected system. With this strategy the success of finding and removing malware depends heavily on the fact that the malware and its signature are known in advance. Because new malwares are constantly developed and spread, new signature definitions must also be developed and distributed by the vendor and installed by the system owner. Otherwise, new types of viruses will not be detected.

Vulnerability Scanners

Vulnerability scanners are special tools designed to automatically find vulnerabilities in systems. Security Administrator Tool for Analyzing Networks (SATAN), designed by Wietze Venema and Dan Farmer, Computerized Oracle and Password System (COPS), proposed by Dan Farmer and Gene Spafford, and ISS (Internet Security Scanner), written by Christopher William Klaus, are all examples of such tools. These tools are intended to be used by the system owner, but they could also be used by an attacker of a system. That these tools can be used as a valuable tool by an attacker has been discussed a lot in the past. Some people are of the opinion that these tools should not be available and distributed to the masses because an attacker can misuse them.

The outcomes of these software packages are typically a list of vulnerabilities present in the system. In some case, fixes are also suggested.

Summary

In this chapter, we have introduced the concept of computer and network security. We started by discussing terminology, then we discussed vulnerabilities and threats. We also introduced the common protection mechanisms used to implement a certain security policy. The topic of the next chapter is the Internet and especially the World Wide Web.

Additional Reading

A fairly large number of textbooks focusing on security are available on the market. Some of them are listed here in alphabetical order. Note, however, that we do not attempt to give a complete list of the literature, but rather a set of books that we use on a regular basis in our daily work.

Chapman, D. Brent, and Elizabeth D. Zwicky. *Building Internet Firewalls*. Sebastopol: O'Reilly & Associates, Inc., 1995.

Denning, Dorothy E. *Information Warfare and Security*. New York: ACM Press, 1999.

Garfinkel, Simon, and Gene Spafford. *Practical UNIX & Internet Security*, 2nd edition. Sebastopol: O'Reilly & Associates, Inc., 1996.

Gollmann, Dieter. *Computer Security*. New York: John Wiley & Sons, Ltd., 1999.

Pfleeger, Charles P. *Security in Computing*, 2nd edition. New Jersey: Prentice-Hall, Inc., 1997.

Stallings, William S. *Cryptography and Network Security*, 2nd edition. New Jersey: Prentice-Hall, Inc., 1999.

CHAPTER 3

The World Wide Web

This chapter is for readers who are unfamiliar with the Internet and especially the World Wide Web (also known as the Web). Here we explain how everything fits together so that the chapters that follow are more accessible to the Internet rookie.

An Introduction to the Internet and the Web

The Internet is a group of millions of computers. It is possible to fetch information from any computer in this group, assuming that the owner of this computer will allow it. To reach the information, a set of protocols is used—that is, rule-sets that specify how information can be sent and received.

One of the most commonly used Internet services besides email is the World Wide Web.[1] Invented in the early 1990s, the Web was and still is the real killer application of the Internet. After the Web's introduction, it took only a few years for the Internet to be the everyday tool for millions of people, in both their professional and private lives, and that number continues to grow. People use the Web of today for many different types of activities, such as banking, trading, making ticket reservations, retrieving information, advertising, gambling, gaming, and holding auctions.

[1] Yet another common name is W3.

An Historic Introduction to the Internet

The Internet first started as a research project, initiated by the Advanced Research Project Agency (ARPA) of the Department of Defense (DoD) in the United States. Basically, the idea was to try to connect computers in a geographically dispersed network. The first version was called ARPANET. In 1972, ARPA became DARPA, and the agency continued to promote the ARPANET project. Later ARPANET evolved from a lab experiment exploring the possibilities of creating a network of a few dispersed computers to a network of interconnected networks—an internet.

Developing an internet in which different kinds of equipment could interact with each other was a big challenge at the time. In 1973-74, researchers designed the Transmission Control Protocol/Internet Protocol (TCP/IP). Originally, TCP/IP was intended to provide support for these requirements:

- Interoperability between heterogeneous systems
- End-to-end communication across a multitude of diverse networks
- Robust and automatic operation in the face of failures of data links

At the time, the applications used were very simple compared to those used today. The most widely used ones were Telnet for remote login, FTP for file transfer, and email.

NOTE

Even though electronic mail was in the original plan for the Internet, it was merely an afterthought.

In the early 1980s, ARPANET was split into two parts—MILNET and ARPANET, for security reasons. The military moved on with MILNET, while research, development, and other sectors stayed on ARPANET.

In the mid-1980s, the National Science Foundation (NSF) in Washington, D.C., put quite a bit of money behind its effort to distribute Internet technology to many universities in addition to the ones already involved, including Berkeley, MIT, Stanford, and UCLA. Soon, the Internet started to spread all over the globe.

In 1990, the DoD decided to disband ARPANET. In its place, the NSFNET backbone, in cooperation with other agency networks, became the principal backbone network of the Internet.

An Introduction to the Web

In 1991, Tim Berners-Lee developed a vision for a Network Information Project at le Centre Européen de Recherche Nucléaire (CERN) in Switzerland. His mission was to create an easy but powerful global information system based on hypertext. Probably the two most important parts that came out of the project were these:

- The HyperText Markup Language (HTML)
- The HyperText Transfer Protocol (HTTP)

HTML is the markup language for publishing information on the Web. When designing HTML, ideas were brought from the Standard Generalized Markup Language (SGML). SGML is a standardized way of organizing and structuring information in a document, or set of documents, and it is further described in Appendix A, together with the Extensible Markup Language (XML).

Although HTML may not be easy for the average person to comprehend, once it is published its use becomes clear. What was once a jumble of words and commands is translated into a concise Web document consisting of text, figures, hyperlinks, and other elements.

HTTP is the other central component from the initial project at CERN. HTTP is a stateless communications protocol based on TCP, originally used to retrieve HTML files from Web servers when it was designed in 1991. Version 1.1 (defined in [RFC2616]) has evolved somewhat; it allows clients and servers to use a multitude of headers to convey state information and user-agent descriptions and serves as a rudimentary means for user authentication. The original version created in 1991, referred to as HTTP version 0.9, is a relatively simple protocol for communication between clients and servers. The most current version of the HTTP protocol is version 1.1.

Both HTML and HTTP have been developed further since the time they were first suggested. The World Wide Web Consortium (W3C), initiated in October 1994 and founded by Tim Berners-Lee, has committed to leading the technical evolution of the Web. Today, the W3C has more than 500 member organizations. Microsoft, IBM, and Ericsson are just a few of the W3C's members.

The Traditional Web Architecture

The two basic components in the Web architecture are the Web browser and the Web server. The Web browser offers a graphic interface to the user and is responsible for communication with Web servers. The communication protocol between the browser and the Web server follows the standardized HTTP protocol that we already covered.

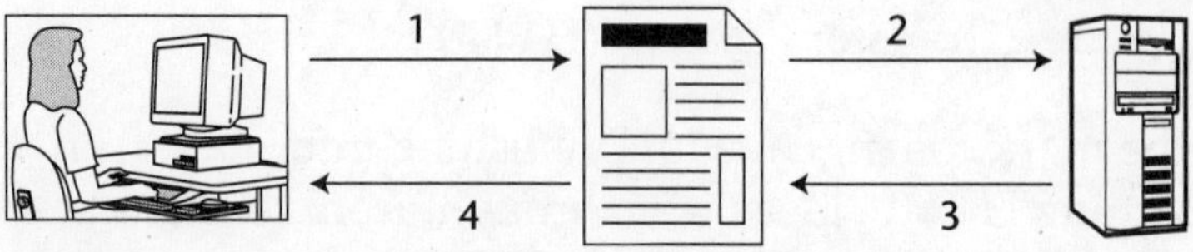

Figure 3.1 An Interaction between a user and a Web server.

Browsing the Internet is often called surfing. Let's take a look at the typical Web surfing scenario, illustrated in Figure 3.1:

1. The user requests a service by clicking on a link or by entering a command with the keyboard. The Web browser catches the command and translates it into an HTTP request.
2. The browser then forwards the newly created request to the Web server of the content provider. When the server receives a request, it starts processing it.
3. When the processing is done, the Web server sends back a response to the browser.
4. When the browser receives a response, it translates it to a human-readable format, giving you the pictures and nice fonts that the Web designer at the originating server had in mind.

The interface between the user and the browser is the standardized language HTML. Between the browser and the server, the communication protocol HTTP is used. Note, however, that Figure 3.1 illustrates just the simplest form of communication between a user and a Web server. Many additional steps might exist along the way, as we see later in this chapter. HTTP is a so-called client/server protocol, which means that the browser is the client and the Web server is the server. In HTTP, a server is normally waiting for client requests. A simple example of a client request is as follows:

```
GET /index.php HTTP/1.1
HOST: WWW.werespectyou.ws
```

- GET is the HTTP method used to retrieve the page.
- /index.php is the file to be retrieved.
- HTTP/1.1 is the version of the protocol that the browser uses.
- www.werespectyou.com is what the client thinks is the server's hostname.

When a server receives a request, data processing starts, and eventually a response is sent back to the client.

```
HTTP/1.1 200 OK
Date: Sat, 26 Jan 2002 21:39:26 GMT
Server: Apache/1.3.20 (Win32)
X-Powered-By: PHP/4.0.6
Connection: close
Content-Type: text/html


<!DOCTYPE html PUBLIC "-//W3C//DTD HTML 4.01 Transitional//EN"
        "http://WWW.w3.org/TR/html4/loose.dtd">
<html>
```

...

- HTTP/1.1 is the version of the protocol used when answered.
- 200 OK on the first line tells the client that the document has been found.
- Date expresses the current date and time in GMT (Greenwich Mean Time) on the server.
- Apache/1.3.20 is the Web server used.
- PHP is a script language used by this particular host.
- Content-type is a message to the receiver about how the content that follows is to be interpreted.
- Document type is HTML.
- Last is the document itself.

A client, on the other hand, waits for the user to give a command. An entered command must always be translated into an HTTP request before it can be forwarded to the server. The browser is responsible for this translation. HTML is the standardized language used by the browser to create the user interface.

To locate a server on the Internet, Universal Resource Locations (URLs) are used. A URL is simply the uniform way to address Web servers on the Internet. A simple example of a URL is this:

http://WWW.test.werespectyou.com:80/dir/subdir/file.cgi?name=greta&age=34

where:

- http:// is the protocol used.
- www.test.werespectyou.com is the domain.
- :80 is the TCP port number on which the Web server is listing.
- /dir/subdir/ is the directory and its subdirectory, relative to the root of the Web server's file structure.
- file.cgi is the file to be retrieved.
- ? is a starter for the GET parameters.
- name=greta&age=34 is the parameters name and age, and their values given this request.

Proxies and Such

An HTTP proxy is a server, which works like this: A Web client may connect to a proxy over HTTP, while passing the URL pointing to the content it wishes to retrieve to that proxy. The proxy then acts as an HTTP client and retrieves the resource from the URL requested by the originating client. When this operation has terminated, the proxy returns the retrieved content to the client.

In many cases, a user on his or her corporate (or internal) network does not directly connect to an outside Web server, due to security or other reasons. In those cases, the proxy acts as a mediator between the browser and the Web server. The proxy to the Web server mediates every request the client makes. The response for each request is then returned along the same path the request came from—that is, through the proxy. An architecture with a client-side proxy is illustrated in Figure 3.2.

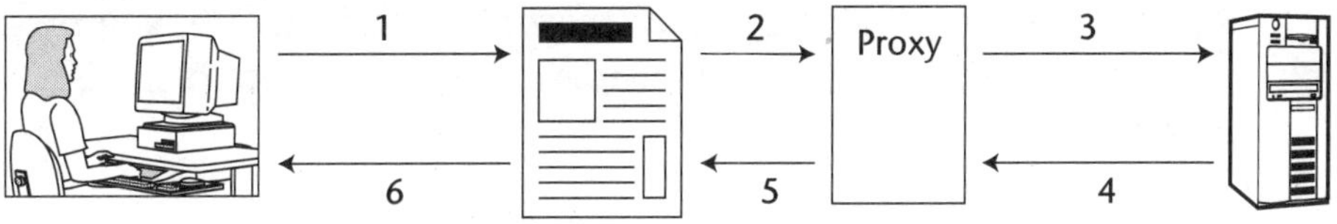

Figure 3.2 An architecture with a client-side proxy.

The difference between the scenarios depicted in Figure 3.1 and Figure 3.2 is that the latter has a proxy between the users on an internal network and the outside, which is normally the Internet. When a proxy is used, all client requests are sent via the proxy to the Web server. The browser now communicates with the proxy (steps 2 and 5 in Figure 3.2), which in turn communicates with the Web server (steps 3 and 4 in Figure 3.2). In many cases, the user is not aware that he or she does not directly communicate with the Web server.

Another common configuration is to have a server-side proxy. In such a case, the proxy is next to the server instead of the client. This implies that the Web server is only indirectly connected to the outside world. All client requests are coming from the proxy, and all server replies are sent back to the proxy, which in turn forwards them to the user.

A combination of the two variants previously mentioned with proxies on both sides is also possible. In this variation, the browser and the Web server are both communicating through their own proxies, both of which are directly connected to each other.

There are essentially two different types of proxies:

- The circuit-level proxy
- The application-level proxy

The basic difference between the two is that a circuit-level proxy is more generic in the sense that it can forward traffic belonging to many different types of application protocols, such as WWW, FTP, Telnet, and email. On the other hand, an application-level proxy can decide which package to forward based on the content of data. It can filter out certain commands in an application protocol, possibly due to the fact that there may be some untrustworthy commands in the protocol. In such cases, the proxy both mediates traffic and restricts the application protocol. This could not be done in a circuit-level proxy because it does not have the ability to understand the traffic sent through it. Note, however, that an application-level proxy can forward only traffic belonging to that specific application.

NOTE

A proxy typically resides on dedicated computers called bastion hosts. These computers are most often installed and configured in the best possible way with respect to security.

Auditing

Auditing, or logging, is the process of storing information about what may have happened in the system. Auditing can be done on many different levels within a computer system. On the operating system level, logging facilities have existed for a long time. Last successful login, last unsuccessful login, last executed command, executed commands, and file system accesses are some examples of the operating system information stored in log files.

Auditing on the application level is also possible. It is especially common to add a logging mechanism to network servers. FTP servers, Telnet servers, email servers, and Web servers all have at least some form of rudimentary mechanism for logging activities on the server side.

Most Web servers could be configured to log incoming http requests. Two types of log configurations can be used:

- Complete logging
- Selective logging

With complete logging, every http request is stored in the log file. With selective logging, the system administrator has specified which types of requests should be stored. Depending on the configuration of the Web server, it is possible that every access from a specified set of domains will always be logged or that certain types of requests, such as GET, might be logged.

Logging is also used to debug erroneous applications, though runtime versions should not contain such messages. They may still exist, especially in companies that develop in-house solutions—that is, where the programmer resides next to the runtime environment.

The Mobile Internet

The mobile Internet is the traditional Internet plus some features that make it possible to access the Internet from a mobile device, such as a phone. The mobile Internet became a viable concept in the late 1990s, and it exists in several forms. The broadest initiative was the Wireless Application Protocol (WAP) founded by Ericsson, Nokia, Motorola, and Unwired Planet (now known as OpenWave). Its standardization body, WAP Forum, has more than 500 members, and it is used by a number of manufacturers.

iMode is a competing concept from NTT Docomo in Japan. It is similar to WAP, but somewhat simpler, which gave it a fast takeoff, and it is the most used technology, though almost only in Japan.

A mobile Internet system consists of a device that uses some kind of gateway or proxy to connect to the Internet. For this kind of device, HTML is not the markup language used because it is not optimized for a device with a yes and no button, a small screen, and limited transmission capabilities. In the case of WAP, the language originally used was WML, but is now XHTML; in the case of iMode, the language used is cHTML.

A number of new services can be offered through mobile Internet, although it has not taken off as some people had hoped. The main reason is that three things need to be in place before any system of this kind can work:

- Users willing to use it
- A network that works reasonably fast and that is not too expensive
- Services and service providers that believe this technology is significant enough to invest in it

In Scandinavia, for example, where mobile Internet could have done well due to the large number of mobile phone users concentrated there, people were not using the services. The problem was not a lack of services: A number of companies, especially those that were late in offering Internet services once and did not want to miss the train again, put out news, stock rates, weather reports, and other abbreviated Web information on WAP sites. Nor was the problem a lack of WAP phones.

The problem was that the services were too simple, slow, and expensive. Almost everyone who had a WAP phone also had a computer that could perform the same functions at a much faster rate and provide better graphics at a lower price. To make them use the mobile Internet, you had to give them something that was not an ugly version of what they could find on the Web, and something that gave them value when they were out there, computerless, with their phone as their only tool to . . . do what? That's the question!

When the mobile Internet takes off, it will not be as a smaller version of the traditional Web, but rather as a new entity that offers different kinds of services. Those services, though based on the same concept and partly on the same network as the Internet, will have different privacy implications.

Summary

This chapter has been a brief introduction to the Internet, where we highlighted features that are of interest in the later chapters. In the next chapter, we take a closer look at these features and at cookies, and we discuss why these are a problem for the privacy-aware user.

CHAPTER 4

Privacy and the Internet

What is actually at risk when we use the Internet? In this chapter, we discuss the risks that the user faces, investigate the user's means for protection, and eventually outline the possible ways to meet the user's demands for protection.

Risks for the Users

What is actually stored or processed, and when can this be a problem?

Log Files and Customer Databases

As soon as a request is made, it is possible to store the user's HTTP header information, together with the requested resource and the parameters. HTTP header information is usually all or some of the following:

- Requested resource—that is, the home page to be retrieved
- Parameters—that is, anything entered in a form or passed on by the link that was followed
- The IP address of the computer or proxy
- The accepted language of the user device
- The user's ID if authentication is used

- The user's device capabilities if:
  - CC/PP or UAProf is used (see Chapter 12)
  - Certain software is installed

Logging one request may not be so harmful, but if everything a user enters is stored, a clickstream pattern can be recognized, which will show how a user used the Web during a specific time period. Listing 4.1 is an example of a Web server log file:

```
141.42.36.41 - - [07/Jan/2002:18:33:14 +0100] "GET
/request/failed/index_failed.htm HTTP/1.0" 404 296
194.237.148.13 - - [08/Jan/2002:10:28:18 +0100] "GET /sub HTTP/1.1" 401
487
194.237.148.13 - hans [08/Jan/2002:10:28:25 +0100] "GET /dat HTTP/1.1"
404 287
194.237.148.13 - hans [08/Jan/2002:10:28:35 +0100] "GET /dat HTTP/1.1"
404 287
194.237.148.13 - hans [08/Jan/2002:10:28:40 +0100] "GET / HTTP/1.1" 200
15290
194.237.148.13 - hans [08/Jan/2002:10:28:40 +0100] "GET
/images/dossier.gif HTTP/1.1" 200 170
194.237.148.13 - hans [08/Jan/2002:10:28:40 +0100] "GET
/images/refresh.gif HTTP/1.1" 200 185
194.237.148.13 - hans [08/Jan/2002:10:28:40 +0100] "GET /images/help.gif
HTTP/1.1" 200 147
194.237.148.13 - hans [08/Jan/2002:10:28:45 +0100] "GET /images/txt.gif
HTTP/1.1" 200 138
```

Listing 4.1 An Apache Web server log file.

Listing 4.1 shows a standard Apache Web server log file. The information shows the IP number of the user's device, the user's ID if basic authentication is used, the time, and which resource was retrieved. Most system administrators use log files like the one in Listing 4.1 to uncover intrusions, and it is important for security reasons that they are allowed to do so. Log files, though, need to be rotated or erased after some time, which is not always the case.

Web applications also usually log information about the user's requests. Security is not usually the reason for doing this because most of the information needed to trace hackers is available in the Web server log files. Instead, debugging can be a reason. If someone—a consultant or an employee—creates an application, and if there is a chance that something might go wrong, the Web designer might keep log files in order to easily go back and see what happened before the problems occurred.

A programmer might keep log files for the first few weeks after creating a new application, then remove the debugging functionality and the log files after seeing that the application works. A careless programmer, though, might never remove them. After a while, the files can contain all sorts of sensitive data about users without anyone's knowing it, and someone else might stumble across these files and realize what value they have.

Web browsers also give away something called the *URL referrer*, which allows a Web server to see the URL of the link you clicked. Some time ago, many flawed, so-called secure Web sites relied on this feature, which authorized access to the home page of other Web sites if and only if the authorization path was on your path of visited links. This is an excellent way to track the user's habits within a site and across domains.

Cookies

Cookies are chunks of information, stored on the user's side. It is possible to store any type of information as long as we stay within the limit of 4 kilobytes, but typically an ID that makes it possible to recognize the user during the session will suffice. Sessions using cookies might be more reliable than sessions based on the TCP/IP session because the external IP number of the user's computer might vary even during a session. Cookies are useful as a tool for creating user-friendly Web applications because they can store user preferences and information so users will not have to redo tasks like registering on a company Web site.

Cookies can be stored permanently. This is a privacy problem because cookies make it possible to recognize a user (or at least the computer that the user uses) between sessions. If roaming profiles are used instead of locally stored cookies, the user can be traced over several computers. To keep Company A from seeing that the user visited Company B, cookies can be retrieved only from the same domain where they were set.

Web Bugs

A Web bug is a transparent image that is normally one-by-one pixel in size. The idea is quite simple—by using the IMG[1] tag's ability to fetch content on a site other than the one you were just visiting, you can "tell" other sites where the user surfs. For more information about HTML and tags in general, see Appendix A. One example is if a site holder wishes advertisers to place an ad at its site, it can place an empty image referring to the potential advertiser at its page:

```
<img src="http://potentialadvertiser.com/webbug.gif" width="1"
height="1">
```

This way, the potential advertiser gets full logs on all the requests that go to the page in question, including IP number and other HTTP header information that comes with a request for an image. To be even more wicked, it is possible to add information to the image retrieval, generated by the host site:

```
<img
src="http://potentialadvertiser.com/webbug.gif?user=greta&email=greta@ga
rbo.net" width="1" height="1">
```

One other way to use Web bugs is by including them in HTML spam. Most HTML-enabled clients will fetch the empty image without asking the user, which will then tell the spammer that the particular message was read, at what time, and even from which particular computer.

Thus, the spam originator can verify which email addresses are real.

You can, of course, achieve the same thing with images that are visible, even if the term Web bug normally refers to invisible pictures. A hacker friend of ours uses a small image of a bug to indicate that he is tracking the users of his sites. The image is generated by a PHP script, which logs everything about that user and sets a cookie. This means that when you go to another one of his sites, it will call the same script, retrieve the cookie, and say "Hey, Hans is surfing under another name through another IP number . . . . Let's log this activity together with all the other stuff that he did yesterday."

Our hacker friend has only a couple of personal sites that are mainly visited by his friends and relatives. Even if his activities are not so appropriate, they are still quite harmless because they are done on a small scale. There are, however, Internet Service Providers (ISPs) that

[1] An IMG tag will insert an image.

collect huge amounts of data, using both invisible Web bugs and quite visible banners, through the same technique.

Spam

Unsolicited messaging and advertising first involved snail mail ads, vacuum cleaner salespeople, and telemarketing. Some five years ago, email spam started to become a real problem, and tomorrow's unsolicited messaging will be through short messages (SMSs) and email sent over mobile Internet. The spam problem, in whatever form it appears, has many angles:

It is a privacy problem (see Chapter 1):

- It is an intrusion into our territory.
- It may be offensive.
- It may be a result of illegitimate data collection and processing.

Spam is time-consuming. It takes time to go through messages and delete them. It also takes time to download them—especially over a mobile connection. They take up space in our computers and mobile devices, and they cost the ISPs money to store, and they literally slow down the Internet.

Spam may be offensive. The content of the messages is not always something we want to read or want our children to read.

Spam can be used for illegal and illegitimate uses. Spammers have used it to spread viruses, false information, and propaganda and to con people into fraudulent deals. For example, on September 12, 2001, several spammers defrauded many people by asking for money to support the relatives of the victims of the September 11 attacks. No one knows how many paid and where the money went. They have also tricked users by making them call a bogus number to unsubscribe from spam mailing lists, where they are charged huge amounts. Sometimes there appears to be no reply at the other end because the spammer has recorded no-answer tones. They sometimes even claim to be someone other than who they are, thus violating the names and reputations of respected companies.

Information Distribution

In order to be spammed, your information would need to have been distributed from the site you visited to some kind of company. This can be done deliberately—for example, the site can sell the information to another organization. It can also be done unintentionally—for instance, an email address is published on the Internet, and a Web crawler run by a spamming organization finds it and stores it. Most of us have received email messages from spammers that sell CDs. They have collected millions of email addresses through such means and use them to send their spam to unsuspecting users.

The following text was taken from an Internet association that aims to help members with benchmarking facilities:

> *The association will also support customer database systems and technology benchmarking efforts:*
>
> - *Research—Access public and private databases.*
> - *Identify study participants—Top companies with customer database systems and technology management organizations.*
> - *Collect data—Manage response collection with the participants as a third party.*
> - *Lead site visits—Structured with best participants.*

Our personal information is a very important asset to companies. A company that sells or otherwise shares information about customers or temporary users with others, though, is not going to remain popular for long.

Tracking

Imagine Hans surfing to various sites. At each site, he gives away different kinds of information. He is convinced that he is anonymous in some cases. All these sites, though, have the same sponsor, belong to the same benchmarking organization, or have another reason to want to share information with a third party. Let's call this third party mordor.com.

All those sites have the same feature, which is a banner/Web bug/regular image, which is in reality a call to a script at mordor.com, with encrypted information, telling mordor.com everything that they know about this user.

```
<img src="http://mordor.com/banner.php?x=AF05BC3D91629DB53074">
```

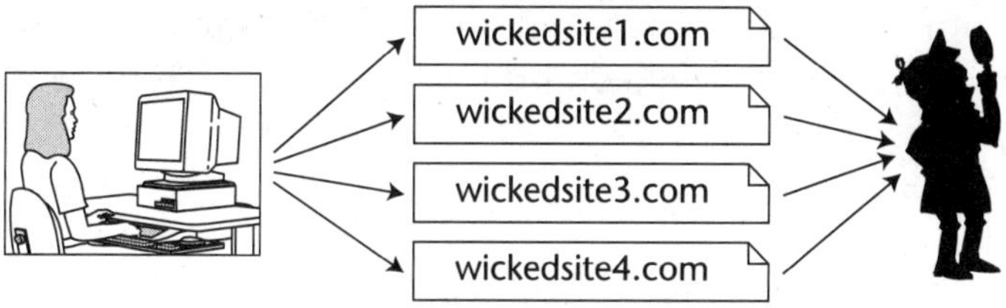

Figure 4.1 The sites contain image links to mordor.com.

mordor.com retrieves Hans's user-agent's request for an image, together with the parameters kindly generated by the hosting site, adding whatever information the site holds on him and the cookie that was set in his computer the last time mordor.com was used, as shown in Figure 4.2.

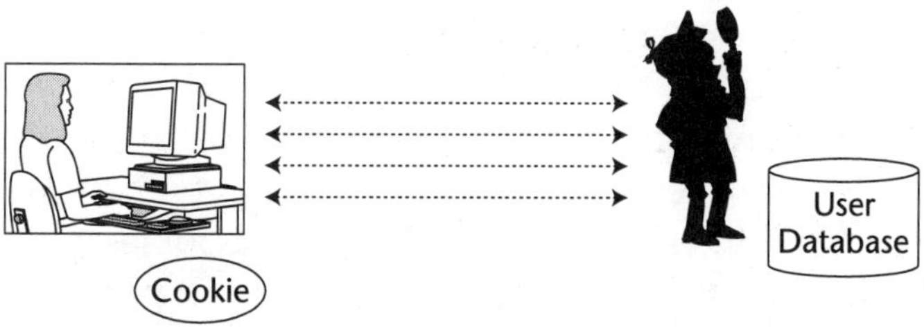

Figure 4.2 Cookies are set and retrieved with the images.

mordor.com stores information about Hans and sends an image back to him, possibly setting a new cookie. Even if he does not allow cookies to be stored, his IP number or other settings sent with the request might help in recognizing him.

What is in it for mordor.com? Well, it might be a benchmarking organization, tracking users for its members, in which case the user behavior can be used for statistical purposes. For example, users who read magazine A are likely to buy clothes at webshop.com and vote a certain way in a survey at the news site news.com.

This may be OK for Hans, who does not care much about privacy. We're all somewhat used to statistics, and in a large group we are anonymous. Now comes the next case.

wickedsite1.com wants to know what kind of ads Hans is interested in. Well, mordor.com tells wickedsite1.com that he regularly visits shoes.com, and now he begins to receive banners with footfetish.com ads. Is this still harmless?

One day, Hans's wife gets tired of the footfetish.com banners she gets every time he borrows her computer, and she hires the well-known divorce detective Shirley Holmes. Guess what her favorite source of information is?

The User Strikes Back

In this section, we place ourselves in the seat of the user, looking at the various means available to deal with the wicked sites.

Lawsuits

Within the United States, legislation is pretty thin in this area. In the European Union, there are harmonized directives on data protection, such as the EU Directive on Dataprotection/Privacy in the Electronic Communication Sector. The directives regulate how companies use personal data collected online—for example, the use of cookies and location information. Still, suing companies for misusing your personal data is hardly ever worthwhile.

Data Alteration

A good way to track what an origin server does to your data is to practice data alteration. Every time data is supplied to a site, it is slightly altered. If your name is Greta Garbo, you can vary this address slightly each time you supply it. For example, you can enter Greta A Garbo, Greta B Garbo, and so on. You can change the address 221b, Baker Street to 221b-1 Baker Street without making the mail carrier too confused to deliver your mail. If you keep a list somewhere that shows which address you entered at which site, it will be easy to track who forwarded your address to whom.

The big privacy threat, though, is not snail mail ads, but spam through email. Never supplying your real email address is a good rule. Keeping a Hotmail or Yahoo address that you use only for data submission is a way to keep your everyday email address clean. This does not help you track the villainous site unless you register a new address each time you enter an email address, which, of course, will be impossible to support after a while.

The ultimate way to handle email address submission is to register a domain, or at least a subdomain, where you have access to all the email addresses possible. Suppose Greta has an email address at work:

greta@job.com

She then registers a domain called garbo.net. When doing so, she gets access to an almost infinite amount of email addresses—that is, anything@garbo.net or rather anything@whatever.garbo.net. She has access to a computer with a fixed IP number, and there she runs a Web mail client that she uses from any computer to read her personal mail. Everything that goes to @garbo.net she sends to the inbox for that address, meaning that every time she supplies an email address to someone that is not a friend or a business associate, she writes something that reminds her of the company's name with the extension @garbo.net.

Figure 4.3 Form filling using data alteration.

If she gets spammed, she will immediately know who passed on her email address. She can also redirect the messages that come to posswick@garbo.net to a spam box that she checks irregularly, or she can completely delete all email messages that come to that address, as shown in Figure 4.3.

A Web bug passing on this information would then look like this:

```
<img
src="http://potentialadvertiser.com/webbug.gif?user=greta%20PW%20Garbo&e
mail=posswick@garbo.net" width="1" height="1">
```

After a while, she may decide to create a specific subdomain only for email addresses that might be spam, like @nospam.garbo.net. That way, garbo.net is kept clean, and she can create inboxes for her family and friends within the main domain.

Cookie Filtering

Cookie filtering tools can be built in, plug-ins, or proxies. They can normally do one or several of the following:

- Disallow all cookies
- Disallow all cookies except
  - Session cookies
  - Cookies set by the domain that you visit—that is, block Web bugs
- Ask for the user's permission to set or send a cookie
- Convert a permanent cookie to a session cookie
- Tell the user when a cookie is being set

Many object completely to the use of cookies. Session cookies, though, are useful, and many applications would be a lot less smooth if they did not have this functionality. Cookies used with caution are the solution to many problems.

It is also important to remember that even if third-party cookies are blocked, the Web bug can still work through the information sent with the parameters.

Figure 4.4 shows the list of sites trying to set cookies through the Internet Explorer 6 cookie filtering tool. The cookies were never set—but what is in the parameters? The devil's in the details. It is very possible that the site, as the first party, may be able to set cookies through the actual filter and collect the information through the parameters by allowing Web bugs and other images to be retrieved from the site.

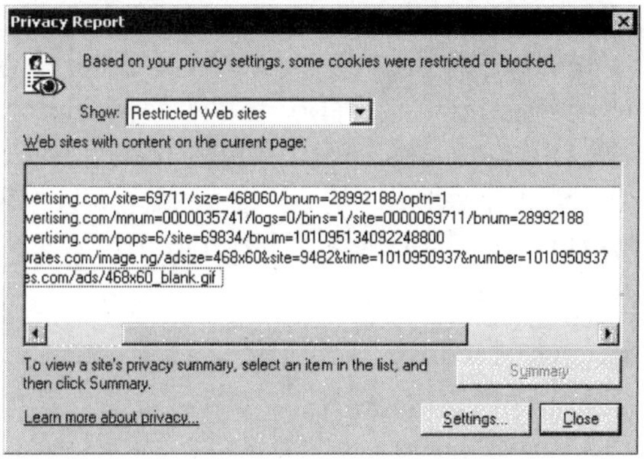

Figure 4.4 User tracking through images.

It is, of course, possible for wickedsite.com not to set the cookie itself. Instead, it can have the first party, specifically the accessed site, set and retrieve the information that it desires, such as a serial number that makes it possible to track the user, and then pass it on through the parameters. This way, it will not even show up in a list like the one in Figure 4.4. The only way the user will know of the other site's existence is if he or she views the HTML source code or uses a specific tool that identifies third-party image retrievals. The chance of discovery is much slimmer.

Without cookies, it is not possible to trace the user over several sites. This is why forbidding third-party cookies would be of great value to the privacy-sensitive user.

Anonymization

In the 1970s, David Chaum wrote a paper on mix nets that described how a user can anonymously access a service, assuming that there was more than one party out there offering mixes that the transmission can pass through. A mix is a piece of software that will route the communication without knowing more than where it came from and where the next destination is; for example, the sender sends to mix1, which directs to mix2, which directs to mix3, which directs to the receiver. Anonymity is preserved through encryption.

In the late 1990s, the Canadian company ZeroKnowledge offered a service called Freedom Network, providing users with the means to use an Internet mix net for anonymous surfing. The mixes were provided by ISPs all over the world, the requests taking different routes every time, and through contracts that ensured no logging and encryption, the user's anonymity was guaranteed. The service, however, was not used enough to be profitable for the company.

Does this prove that users do not want anonymity? That users want it if they do not have to pay for it? Or that users do not want to complicate life by getting yet another subscription? We do not know, but it is an interesting use case.

Trusted Parties

We discussed trust in the first chapter. Solutions based on the trust of the user are becoming very popular. The idea is simple: One party, someone who you believe will never compromise your data, handles your relations to other parties.

The advantage is obvious. A big company with a good name that acts as a trusted third party has much to lose from misbehaving. The disadvantage, however, is that when one company acts as an aggregation point for all our requests, the privacy risks are much greater. We have already discussed clickstreams and the knowledge that you can draw from having a big mass of information.

Those trusted third parties will probably not spam you—that would be suicide. Targeted advertisement and telemarketing as a result of data mining, though, will probably escape the user's detection. When selecting a trusted third party, it is wise to review its privacy policy very thoroughly.

Identities

What is an identity? For most people, it is the information that dictates who a person is. In this context, it is information, or fragments of information, that relate to a person. These fragments may or may not be enough to truly identify the person. For example, at work your identity is your login alias and, we hope, a few other things. To the bank, you are several bank account numbers. In a survey, you are a woman, 32, with two children. At your favorite love-search site, you are Lolita, 25. An identity that is either incorrect or insufficient to describe you as a physical person is referred to as an alias or a pseudonym. At the door of your office, your identity is a chunk of data on a plastic card—your nameplate.

Following are a few definitions:

- Anonymization means supplying no identity or identifiable information at all.
- Pseudonymization means using a false or insufficient identity for a specific user.
- Identification means discovering someone's—or something's—identity.
- Authentication means proving your identity—either it is sufficient or insufficient to describe you as a physical person. Authentication implies identification but includes the aspect of provability.
- Authorization means using your identity given a specific context to grant you access to a service. Authorization implies authentication, though we must remember that it is not necessarily your full identity that is given away—only the identity that you use for the request.

In a Single Sign-On (SSO) system, a user authenticates himself or herself once to a set of services and is able to use all the services within this service domain without further authentication.

Privacy in a Mobile Internet

In future mobile Internet services, privacy will be a much greater issue than in traditional Web environments. The personal data that will pass through a mobile Internet system contains more information, such as location data and device capabilities.

Let's take a look at the features of a mobile Internet browser compared to a standard Web browser:

- It has a small screen, which means that it is difficult to view a lot of information at the same time.
- The connection is slower, which means that there is an advantage to limiting the amount of data sent.
- It has a physical location, either in the device itself (that is, GPS) or the location data that can be retrieved from the operator.

- It has limited input facilities, compared to a PC with a keyboard.
- It is personal, and its device capabilities tell you much, or at least some things, about its owner.

All those features call for personalized services, which in turn require profiling the user, which in turn requires collection of user and device data. Add to the previous list new features that will help with using the device as a bonus or payment card, identity card, door opener, and all the other stuff promised by those in the telecom business, and you can see that there will be lots of transactions and lots of data floating around through the cables of the Internet world. That data will be stored and processed in huge databases to provide the end user with adjusted content so that he or she will be interested in continuing to use the services.

The means for protection are the same as in the traditional Web environment, though much more critical. We want to make another point at this stage as well: There is a need for a tool that allows transmission of data according to the wishes of the user.

The key to future mobile Internet services is to create a user-friendly way to put the user in charge of his or her privacy preferences.

Summary

In this chapter, we have discussed the privacy risks for Internet users and what can be done from the user's side to eliminate those risks and enhance privacy on the Web. In the next chapter, we introduce P3P and discuss how it differs from other privacy-enhancing technologies.

CHAPTER 5

Platform for Privacy Preferences Project

The World Wide Web Consortium (W3C), whose goal is to "lead the World Wide Web to its full potential by developing common protocols that promote its evolution and ensure its interoperability," formed the initiative for the Platform for Privacy Preferences Project (P3P) in 1997. Its goals, as worded by Tim Berners-Lee, founder of the Web, are to find a technical way to achieve the following:

- Personal choice and informed consent
- Commitment from publishers about use of data

The technology should also provide a basis to enforce legislative actions if publishers on the Web do not adhere to their own statements.

P3P and Legislation

P3P has different legal implications in the United States and in Europe. In the United States, P3P can be used to make a picky end user trust you because if you do not do what you say, you can be sued—in essence, you would be breaking a contract. We would need to provide users with a way to establish a contract with the server they want to communicate with, and if the server breaks the contract, it will be possible to claim liability. If the user does not care about privacy, never mind.

Within the European Union, P3P might in the future be used to get the user's prior informed consent so that you can do things to the user's data that are not normally allowed by law. There are several European Commission directives on data protection, including EU Directive 95/46/EC, on the protection of individuals with regard to the processing of personal data and on the free movement of such data, and EU Directive 97/66/EC, concerning the processing of personal data and the protection of privacy in the telecommunications sector. These two are the most relevant to privacy in the IT sector. The directives are to be implemented in the legislation of the member countries; if member countries have specific needs, those can also be reflected. For example, in Sweden each citizen has a "person-number," a unique identifier formed by the date of birth in six digits plus four digits. The ninth digit is even for women and odd for men, and the tenth digit is a checksum. This number may not be used in Swedish computer systems unless it's necessary, and specific precautions have been taken for protection. Due to the extended European privacy legislation, we argue that P3P is not really necessary to protect the European user, unless this user has more specific privacy demands than is covered by law.

However, P3P can be a useful tool for the content provider. For example, as a content provider, legislation gives you a number of different rules that limit your legal rights to collect and process personal data. All legislation, though, has a back door; it says that "you cannot . . . unless you have the *prior informed consent*" of the user. What is "prior" in this context? Well, something that happens before you act. What is "informed"? It means "read and understood, beyond reasonable doubt." What is "consent"? It is saying "I do."

Thus, if there is a way for a content provider to inform the user about *what would happen* to the user's data if provided, *before* the user provides it and the things do happen, and if the user gives consent, then it is legal to do almost anything.

Two issues need to be raised here. The first is that while we are writing this, there has not yet been a law case in any country where the legal implications of a "P3P contract" have been tried. Thus, what we just stated about P3P in the United States and Europe is still hypothetical, though it is a reasonable hypothesis.

The other issue is that the world does not consist of the European Union and the United States alone. This book does not contain any more information about the various laws in all countries of the world. This is a book on technical issues. Regardless of how you choose to use P3P, the advice is this: Make sure that you do what you say you do, for legal, ethical, and PR reasons. Lying will cost you in one way or another, regardless of the location of your server or company.

How to do what you say you do is discussed in the following chapters. Reading a book about how to create a policy takes 10 minutes. Discussing the legal implications of P3P is nearly impossible because the technology is too young. Designing your Web site for the privacy-aware end user and then making the user aware of that in a P3P policy will really make a difference in the competition for users in the new generation of the Web.

P3P Scenario

The actors in a P3P agreement are the content provider and the user; however, the user is not supposed to have to do anything. The user has an agent acting on his or her behalf, called a user-agent, which knows what the user wants. The agent is a piece of software.

Let's consider the following scenario: Greta wants to retrieve the resource http://werespectyou.com/catalogue/page5.html, but only if the site owner promises not to pass on her IP number to other parties.

Retrieve the P3P Policy File

The first mission in this scenario is to provide the user Greta with a policy before any HTTP request is sent. Sending an HTTP request to get the policy file does this.

Question: How do you send a request to get a policy before you send a request?

Answer: You do not. We have a problem here.

Problem: We want a policy, but we do not want to send a request for this policy because we know from Chapter 2 and Chapter 3 what large amounts of data can be redrawn from a request.

Solution: We create a safe zone, like a no-man's land, where the mutual understanding between the parties is "we do not really know each other yet, so let's pretend this communication does not take place."

The safe-zone in P3P is the phase before we have an actual agreement. The idea is that the user-agent sends as little information about the user as possible, and the content provider processes and stores no information about the user.

Thus, the problem is solved. The user-agent can safely—more or less—ask for a policy file.

Now, assume that werespectyou.com has published a lot of retrievable pages, images, and files. Some of these resources use forms that the user can fill in, while others are considered more important and all HTTP header information is logged forever when this page is retrieved. In this case, it is not wise of werespectyou.com to publish one single policy file for all resources.

Problem: How do we publish several policies and tie each resource to a specific policy file?

Solution: We create a reference file, like a site map, where we map each resource to a policy file.

Next problem: How do we find this reference file?

There are three answers to this, but for simplicity we use only the simplest and most typical one in this scenario. The other two are explained in Chapter 9.

Solution: We determine a specific, so-called well-known, location at each Web site where the reference file can be found: /w3c/p3p.xml.

Thus, the well-known location of werespectyou.com is http://werespectyou.com/w3c/p3p.xml. The decision by the P3P group to reserve this Uniform Resource Identifier (URI) was not without controversy. It is a simple solution, though, to a problem that in any other way would have been more or less complex.

Coming this far in the scenario, we can now complete the first mission, to retrieve the policy file, by stating that Greta's user-agent must do the following:

1. Send an HTTP request for http://werespectyou.com/w3c/p3p.xml while disclosing as little information as possible in the HTTP headers.
2. Within the reference file, look up the policy file that matches /catalogue/page5.html.
3. Get the appropriate policy file while still not disclosing more than necessary.

Retrieve the Preferences

The second mission is to make sure that the user's wishes match the policy file. This is actually the trickiest part, in our opinion. How does a machine determine what its master user wants?

Not all user-agents attempt to do this. Some contain a viewer that presents the P3P policy file only in human-readable format, such as English. If the goal is to perform the agreement with the site without bothering Greta, the user-agent must have a notion of the user's wishes and be able to act upon them.

The user's wishes, a set of rules, are called preferences. They can be stored in a machine-readable format called APPEL (A P3P Preference Exchange Language), specifically designed for this purpose. If the preferences are stored in APPEL, the user-agent only needs to match the P3P policy file with the APPEL file, then request the resource, block the resource, or prompt the user.

The problem is how to get the user's preferences into the APPEL file. The point is not to disturb the user. There are several ways.

Default Settings

Default settings—that is, the settings that the user-agent makes before the user actually starts using it—are not really what we would call the user's preferences. There must be some idea of which preferences should be the default for each agent. As we are writing this, there are only experimental P3P user-agents out there, so we cannot be of much help here. Still, if you read this some time after 2002, you should find out what the default settings of the most frequently used user-agents are and make sure that you adhere to them as closely as possible.

We assume that system administrators will be able to configure these settings too, just as they fix security levels for their users. As we have been arguing through the last three chapters, privacy is not a company policy; it is a fundamental human right. The right to choose is a personal, ethical standpoint, and having anything called "default" in this context is somewhat repelling.

Administration Tools

All user-agents must, of course, provide their master user with an administration tool to enter the privacy settings. We imagine that they will look something like this:

- I agree to provide my IP assuming that you agree not to pass it on.
- I agree to fill in a form with personal data, if you promise not to store my email address.

The various options for the user are immense. Explaining them in a way that is understandable for anyone who is not an engineer is a true challenge. Because there is a possibility that the user's stored preferences will have legal implications in some countries, such as enforcing the user's "prior informed consent," it is not only a matter of making the administration tool good enough in the opinion of the user-agent–makers. It is important that the lead text that precedes the storage of a preference is understandable enough to hold up in court.

As said before, this is not something we know today, but it is something we strongly believe will happen.

The greatest problem with administration tools is apparently that very few people will actually take the trouble to use them.

"Remember This Decision"

A user's preferences, whether they are privacy preferences or any other kind of preferences, are usually not stored as default or through administration interfaces. They are stored by having the system learn while the computer or system is being used.

We have all seen "remember this decision" check boxes and are familiar with how they work:

1. The user tries to do something.
2. The system is not sure how to react.
3. The system asks a question, followed by a check box, saying "remember this decision."
4. If the check box is checked, the decision will be stored—that is, the decision will become a "preference."

We expect P3P-enabled user-agents to rely heavily on this kind of feature when building up a preference database. The decisions along the way will be the rules that the user-agent acts on when performing the agreement.

One question raised but not yet answered within the European Union is this: Can P3P be used to achieve the user's informed consent? If a user-agent reads the policy and accepts it to get the content that follows the policy, does this action count as the user having given consent for the data processing that is about to take place?

Just to give you an idea of the complexity of this issue, another related question is this:

"Does it matter whether the remember-this-decision check box is checked or unchecked before the user clicks OK? Must the user actively check the box himself or herself, or can the system check it for the user?"

If you are one of the implementers of the future P3P-enabled user-agents, we wish you luck in solving these issues. Creating an APPEL preference file is the easiest thing. Combining the ethical and legal aspects of the texts and message boxes that precede the user's choices with common usability features is the greatest challenge. For most of us, though, the preferences are just there, in the user-agent.

Perform the Agreement

Thus, in our user scenario, the user-agent now has a set of preferences and a policy file, and it is time to match them with each other. In this phase the user-agent can run into trouble, assuming that the P3P policy file is incorrect, according to the P3P schema. The best way to deal with this is to make sure that the file is correct. If it is not, a user-agent is supposed to discover this and act on it, by refusing to act on it.

This is important. Often, markup languages are used for formatting. This is the case with HTML, WML, MathML, and a number of other MLs. The most complex part of the parsers—that is, the software that interprets these languages—is to try to figure out how to correct erroneous markup code so that the content will be displayed as desired by the person who once created it.

When it comes to a policy file created in a machine-readable format, the parser should *not* do this. Corrections could cause the user-agent to act in a way that is not consistent with the desires of the user, and then the whole purpose is somewhat forlorn. The tasks of the user-agent are to do the following:

1. Parse the policy file.
2. Determine whether it is correct—that is, that it follows the XML schema published for P3P.
3. Compare it with the user's preferences.
4. Act.

What actions are to be taken is pretty much up to user-agent, but the typical action would be to get the required resource if all's well and tell the user about the inconsistencies in the site's policy if this is not the case. The message about the inconsistencies should preferably be accompanied by a question about whether to get the site anyway, such as this:

"This site will sell your HTTP header information to third-party companies. Do you still want to get the resource?" While the user-agent is still bothering its master user with a question like this, it might as well throw in a remember-this-decision check box, so that it will not have to ask the next time.

The P3P Agreement

Whereas the previous scenario was meant to be a crash course in how a P3P agreement works, we now look at the procedure a little more closely. In the next chapter, we discuss in detail how the reference and policy files are created, and in Chapter 8 we take a closer look at P3P user-agents and other tools.

In the scenario depicted in Figure 5.1, we have deliberately removed the user entirely. The user performs one action, which is to request a page. The rest of the actions are preferably performed without the user's interference.

The user can have any kind of device. In Chapter 12, we discuss privacy in the mobile Internet in detail and how P3P can be used to protect much more data than in the traditional Web. For now, let's just state that Internet access is not limited to a connected PC, but that many other devices can connect the same way.

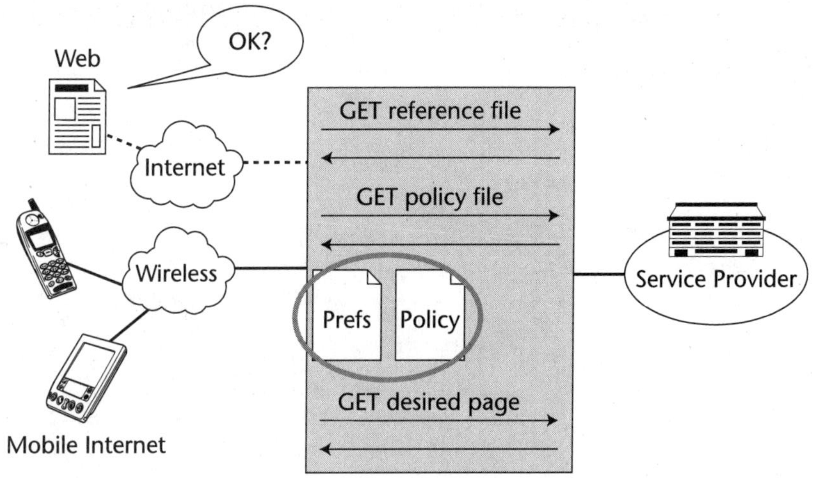

Figure 5.1 A P3P agreement.

If the user-agent is of the kind that is expected to act on the user's behalf and not just a P3P viewer, the user has stored preferences in an APPEL file where the user-agent can retrieve them. This is apparently not totally necessary because normally the only party that will read the preferences is the user-agent itself, but there are advantages to using APPEL:

- It is already defined, meaning somebody else has done the thinking.
- There are already tools developed for comparison with a P3P policy file.
- If the user wants to transport his or her preferences to some other environment, using a standardized format is beneficial.

There is one drawback, though: The language is not optimized with regard to storage or parse time. Nor is there any available graphical user interface (GUI) for creation. If the user-agent is a proxy at a third party that holds the preferences of many users, it is probably wiser to keep the preferences in a database. If the user-agent is a constrained device, such as a mobile phone, it might be better to store the preferences in some proprietary, optimized binary code.

The task of the content provider is to store two files on the site:

- One reference file, at the well-known location
- One policy file that is pointed to by the reference file

```
<?xml version="1.0" ?>
<META xmlns="http://www.w3.org/2000/12/P3Pv1">
  <POLICY-REFERENCES>
    <POLICY-REF about="http://werespectyou.com/w3c/policy.xml">
      <INCLUDE>/*</INCLUDE>
    </POLICY-REF>
  </POLICY-REFERENCES>
</META>
```

Listing 5.1 A P3P reference file.

In the reference file in Listing 5.1, we can see that the policy file named policy.xml, stored in the /w3c folder, together with the reference file, presumably, is valid for all resources at werespectyou.com because there is an include tag containing /* and no exclude tag. We can also see that the reference file is of the type P3P version 1 from the second line.

```
<?xml version="1.0"?>
<POLICY xmlns="http://www.w3.org/2000/12/P3Pv1" discuri="http://were-
spectyou.com/privacy/policy.html">
  <ENTITY>
    <DATA-GROUP>
      <DATA ref="#business.name">werespectyou.com</DATA>
      <DATA ref="#business.contact-info.postal.city">Metropolis</DATA>
    </DATA-GROUP>
  </ENTITY>
  <ACCESS>
    <contact-and-other/>
  </ACCESS>
  <STATEMENT>
    <PURPOSE>
      <admin required="always"/>
```

Listing 5.2 A P3P policy file.

```
    </PURPOSE>
    <RECIPIENT>
      <ours/>
    </RECIPIENT>
    <RETENTION>
      <indefinitely/>
    </RETENTION>
    <DATA-GROUP>
      <DATA ref="#dynamic.miscdata" optional="no">
        <CATEGORIES>
        <computer/>
        </CATEGORIES>
      </DATA>
    </DATA-GROUP>
  </STATEMENT>
</POLICY>
```

Listing 5.2 *(continued)*

The policy file in Listing 5.2 is a very simple one, stating the following:

- A natural language—for example, English—version of the policy can be found at /privacy/policy.html.
- The name of the business is "werespectyou.com," and the company is located in Metropolis.
- If the user asks for what information the content provider has stored, access will be granted.
- For system administrative reasons, the HTTP log files (here called dynamic misc-data) are stored, and the content provider cannot say for how long (that is, there are no routines for log file removal).
- Nobody else gets access to these files because the recipient is "ours."

When using Microsoft Internet Explorer 6, this really short P3P policy results in the privacy report shown in Figure 5.2.

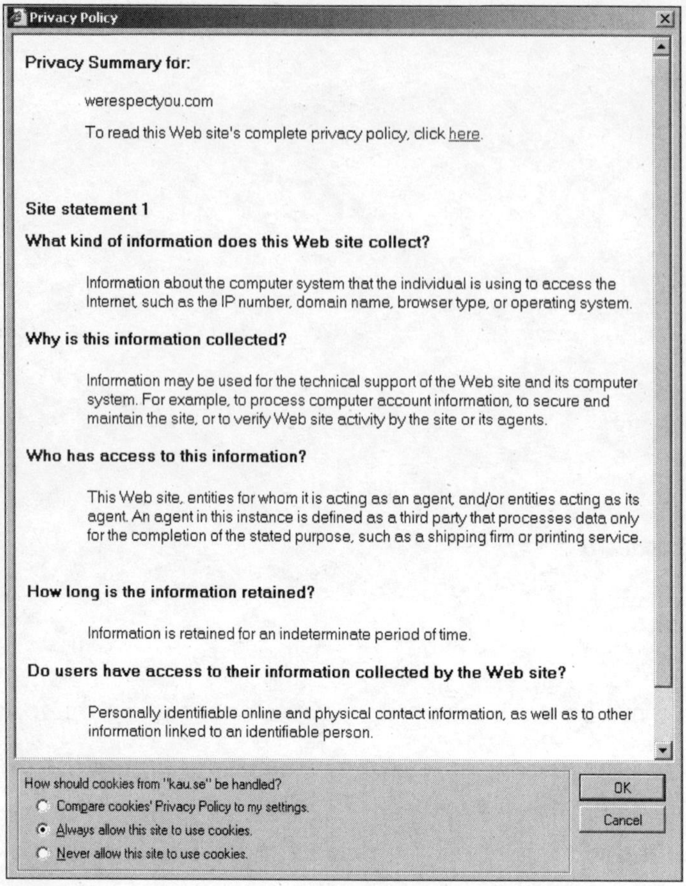

Figure 5.2 An Internet Explorer 6 privacy report.

To perform an agreement on behalf of the user, the policy file will not be run through a viewer, but through a comparison tool, where the file is matched with the user's preferences (Listing 5.3):

```
<appel:RULESET xmlns:appel="http://www.w3.org/2001/02/APPELv1"
xmlns:p3p="http://www.w3.org/2000/12/P3Pv1">
  <appel:RULE behavior="block">
    <p3p:POLICY>
```

Listing 5.3 An APPEL rule-set.

```
        <p3p:STATEMENT>
          <p3p:DATA-GROUP>
            <p3p:DATA ref="#dynamic.miscdata">
            </p3p:DATA>
          </p3p:DATA-GROUP>
          <p3p:RECIPIENT appel:connective="or">
            <p3p:public/>
            <p3p:delivery/>
            <p3p:unrelated/>
          </p3p:RECIPIENT>
        </p3p:STATEMENT>
      </p3p:POLICY>
    </appel:RULE>
  </appel:RULESET>
```

Listing 5.3 *(continued)*

This APPEL rule-set tells us that this particular user-agent will block all requests where the dynamic.miscdata, equal to HTTP request-related information, is delivered to other parties, as is the case when the RECIPIENT tag is set to public, delivery, or unrelated.

Because the P3P policy file in Listing 5.2 contained only an "ours" tag inside the recipient tag, the blocking will not take place, but the page can be requested.

Summary

The P3P concept includes privacy policy files written in an XML-based language specified by the World Wide Web Consortium, preference files written in APPEL, specified by a P3P specification subgroup, and a set of rules (that is, a protocol) for policy retrieval and agreement. The P3P protocol does not in itself say how the user-agent should act on the outcome of the agreement.

In the next chapter, we discuss how to enhance your Web site's privacy before creating a policy.

CHAPTER 6

Enhance Your Web Site's Privacy

In this chapter, we discuss what measures should be taken to enhance a Web site's privacy. We use the EU directive 95/46/EC on the protection of individuals with regard to the processing of personal data and on the free movement of such data as a starting point. Regardless of whether your server is located within the European Union, the directive sheds light on the issues that need to be considered.

Throughout this chapter, we use the term *Europe* to designate member states of the European Union. Of course, there are countries in Europe that are not part of the union, and many member states have not yet implemented the directive in their legislation, even though they should have. There might also be variations in the interpretation of the directive among member states.

Lawfulness and Processing

The general rules on the lawfulness of processing personal data include the following:

- Fair and lawful processing.
- Purpose specification and purpose binding—implying that the purpose must be specified and stuck to.

- Necessity principle—that is, it must be necessary to perform the collection and processing given the specified purpose.
- Accuracy principle—incorrect or illegally stored information must be deleted or corrected.
- Retention—data must not be stored any longer than necessary.
- Right to information—a user should be able to get information about what personal data is being stored.
- Adequate security mechanisms.

Fair and Lawful

The directive[1] *states that member states shall provide that personal data must be processed fairly and lawfully.*

Within states and countries that have data protection directives in their laws, it is, of course, necessary to make sure the law is upheld. There should be supervising bodies and sanctions for those who do not do as they should.

When you begin the process of making your Web site privacy-enhanced, you must start by finding out what is stored and processed. This may not be so easy. Here is where to look:

- Ask the system administrator what is logged. Remember Web server log files and firewall log files.
- Ask the programmers who created the software if debug messages are being left anywhere.
- Take a look at the database, and go through the data model.
- Ask the statistics department if any data mining tools or other tools are being used.

Purpose Specification

Personal data must be

collected for specified, explicit, and legitimate purposes and not further processed in a way incompatible with those purposes. Further processing of data for historical, statistical, or scientific purposes shall not be considered as incompatible provided that member states provide appropriate safeguards.

[1] EU directive 95/46/EC on the protection of individuals with regard to the processing of personal data

Whenever there is a need for data collection and processing, there is also a purpose. This purpose should be stated somehow. A purpose does not necessarily have to benefit the end user, nor does it need to be particularly noble.

Some examples of purposes are these:

- Provide the user with a better experience.
- Conduct demographic surveys.
- Be able to communicate with the end user.
- Perform security auditing.
- Sell user names and email addresses to advertisers.

Also check whether all the cookies being set for data collection are really necessary. Maybe the same thing can be done without cookies, or maybe the purpose of the cookies is not really worthwhile.

After the purpose is specified, it should determine the steps to come. It might sometimes be appealing to reuse data that is already there. For example, data is reused for these purposes:

- Statistics retrieval from security log files
- Emailing users who provided their email addresses
- Selling the customer database

In Europe, this is permitted only if the user is informed about the change of purpose or if the data is anonymized and the user is no longer identifiable.

The first step when making your Web site privacy-enhanced is to clarify where you would store personal data and why you would want to store it. Also try to imagine any future purpose for which you might want to use it because these are not lightweight decisions. The handling of privacy is very much part of the company image, and a contradiction could really hurt the entire organization. This is why the purpose should be aligned with the company policy and external message.

Necessity Principle

Processing and storage of personal data must be

> *adequate, relevant, and not excessive in relation to the purposes for which they are collected and/or further processed.*

We have a purpose for the processing and storage of personal data. Now, it is time to take a look at whether it is really necessary to have all that data, assuming this particular purpose. Are the Web server log files excessive? Is there any specific data being processed that could be removed?

One could wonder about all those Web sites that ask for your gender and age. What do they want with that information? How are the statistics used? We always question everything that we are asked for. It is a good exercise to do so when surfing—when you think as a privacy-aware user, you will not have any problems realizing which problems need to be solved.

Most of all, you should ask yourself whether the user profiles being built are actually going to be used anywhere. Remember that both data that contains the user's name and address and data that could be connected with the user, such as Web server log files, should not be included.

What is really necessary is, of course, a matter of convenience. To be extreme, it is never necessary to use the Internet at all—we have snail mail, grocery stores, and newspapers. One could argue whether personalization is really necessary. Nothing horrible will happen if the user is not able to create his or her own links in a portal, and nothing horrible will happen if the Web page does not say "Hello, Greta." This is why, when possible, you should give the user several possibilities.

Many Web sites use persistent cookies to keep track of a user throughout a session. If you never use the cookies to recognize the users throughout several sessions, you might as well make them temporary. If the cookies are used to recognize the user throughout the sessions, you should ask yourself which one of your purposes this serves.

Right to Correction

Data must be

> *accurate and, where necessary, kept up to date; every reasonable step must be taken to ensure that data that is inaccurate or incomplete, having regard to the purposes for which it was collected or for which it is further processed, is erased or rectified.*

The implication of this requirement from a Web perspective normally means that if the user wants you to remove data, you should do so. To do this, the right means must exist to make it possible. Is it not likely that someone will call you and ask you to remove your Web server log files? You should be prepared to make changes to your user database upon request.

If your Web site has user registration, the best way is to make sure that the user can alter the data at any point. Access to a user profile should include not only the data that the user entered but also data that was collected through other means. Also make sure that the user can delete himself or herself—that is, the user can remove all data related to him or her. This is a feature that is very rarely provided for some reason.

Nobody knows if sites that provide means for profile deletion actually perform this action all the way. Is the profile actually removed from the database, or is it only invisible to me? Are dumps or dif files stored somewhere that can restore the user profile if needed? These are issues that should not be forgotten in the process.

Retention

Data must be

> *kept in a form that permits identification of data subjects for no longer than is necessary for the purposes for which the data was collected or for which it is further processed. Member states shall lay down appropriate safeguards for personal data stored for longer periods for historical, statistical, or scientific use.*

It is not so difficult to adhere to this requirement. When the purpose has expired, the data should be deleted or made anonymous, but this is almost never done. Ask any system administrator when the various log files are deleted, and you will get the answer "when they are too big" or "never." How long do you need to preserve the log files in order to make sure that security is handled in an appropriate way? We suggest that you preserve the files for six weeks. If you have not discovered an intrusion by then, nothing probably happened. Of course, this depends on various factors.

It is not difficult to create a script that erases the records in a flat file that are older than six weeks. On a Linux/Solaris platform, the log rotate functionality can be used.

When should a user be deleted from a customer database? Should the user be erased after not using the site for a certain number of months? How long should records of purchases be kept? Is it necessary to know this year that the user bought a lamp last year? Maybe the user will be offended and think you do not have your computer system in order if you do not have a good system recollection of old transactions. The best way to handle this is to ask users what they want.

Right to Information

> *Whereas, if the processing of data is to be fair, the data subject must be in a position to learn of the existence of a processing operation and, where data is collected from him or her, must be given accurate and full information, bearing in mind the circumstances of the collection.*

You must be able to present the data collected to the end user when asked to do so. This is easily handled if you have an administration page, where the user can go over his or her profile and erase or change whatever he or she wants.

In general, security log files with IP numbers are not included—if you ask about your logged HTTP requests, you should get an answer as to how often log files are cleared, but no one can really require that they be erased or even presented.

All other information must be presented to the user if required, so if there is no administration tool, you must still have the ability to present the information to the user if asked for in, for example, a phone call or an email.

Security

Adequate security mechanisms must be used to make sure that no intruders get access to the personal data. This also goes for internal intruders. The questions you must ask yourself are these: Who has access to the data? Do these people understand that this information must be handled with utmost care?

Even though a company board has all the best intentions, it does not help if the message is not communicated to the personnel. Sometimes a special lock to the room with the database is enough, but it is also important that everybody does not have access to the log files and database.

Security intrusions, of course, also include hacking your way through firewalls and reading, changing, or even destroying sensitive data.

It is also a security intrusion to enter another user's account. Thus, weak authentication schemes are a serious privacy problem.

Checklist

The following is a checklist for Web site owners when enhancing the privacy at your sites.

- ❑ Summarize where user data is stored or processed.
  - ❑ Remember all the log files.
  - ❑ Check debugging messages.
  - ❑ Check the database used.
- ❑ Determine why the information is used.
- ❑ Make sure you actually need all that personal data. Can you perform the same function with less information?
  - ❑ If possible, provide the user with several options, where the loss in privacy is compensated by other gains.
- ❑ Is it possible to easily retrieve all the information that is stored about a specific user, on the user's demand?
- ❑ Is it possible to easily delete or update this information?
- ❑ Is it even possible to provide registered users with the means to easily update their profiles, including their privacy settings?
- ❑ Is data deleted at the moment it is not needed anymore?
  - ❑ How long are log files stored?
  - ❑ When are registered users removed from the system?
  - ❑ If a user chooses to unregister, is the user removed from the system or only marked as inactive?

- Are adequate security mechanisms handled?
  - Do only the personnel who need to have access to the personal information actually have it?
  - Are all risks of external intrusions eliminated?
  - Is it difficult to access another user's account?

Summary

In this chapter, we discussed the different aspects of privacy, through a European perspective. We also have provided a checklist that you can use to see how your Web site handles privacy.

In the next chapter, we give an overview of privacy policies.

CHAPTER 7

Five Steps to Creating a Privacy Policy

In this chapter, we describe how to create a privacy policy in five distinct steps:

1. Create a written privacy policy for the site in a natural language, such as English.
2. Decide which part of the policy applies to which Web pages.
3. Create a P3P policy.
4. Create a policy reference file in which the different policies are mapped to their respective pages.
5. Evaluate the policies.

Step 1—Create a Written Privacy Policy for the Site

The first step in making a P3P-compliant privacy policy for a site is to create a written privacy policy in a natural language. One reason for creating a policy in such a language is that not everyone involved is or needs to be acquainted with P3P syntax. P3P is, like any other computer-readable language, formalized, and to make a full statement, the nuances of a natural language are needed.

Another reason is that according to the P3P specification, a human-readable version of the P3P policy should, and sometimes must, be used to further inform users about the policies used on the site. Thus, you will need to have both.

When data that can be related to an individual is collected, it is important to explicitly note the following:

- Which data is collected
- Why this data is collected
- Who can access the collected data
- How long the collected data will be kept

From the previous chapter, we know that personal data should not be collected without a purpose. We also learned that performing the collection and processing is needed to perform the respective tasks—that is, there should not be any other, less privacy-intrusive way of performance.

Step 2—Decide Which Policies Apply to Which Pages

The next step in making a Web site P3P compliant is deciding which part of the written policy created in Step 1 applies to which Web pages. Most sites have more than just one Web page, and different data collection strategies could be applicable.

Often, a site is divided into a part open to the public and a subscription-based part. Within the public part, it is quite possible that the only data collection used is security log files. The site might also have a part where users can log in. By providing data about themselves, the users will get something back. The site will typically have the user create an account where as much information as possible is collected. This could be name, age, address, email address, areas of interest, type of occupation, and marital status. After the user gets a subscription, services are open to the user.

You may also want to have a separate policy for separate pages if the site sells goods. In this case, there might be three types of policies: one for users who want just to look around, one where an account for buying things is used, and one for the page where the user supplies payment and delivery information.

It is also possible that one domain hosts several other sites, like a mall, in which case each part will have one or several policies.

Step 3—Create P3P Policies

At this point, we have a written policy in a human-readable language and information about which part of the policy to apply to which page. The next step is to create one or more P3P policies. The documents produced in Step 1 and Step 2 are input at this stage. You can find the current P3P specification at http://www.w3.org/TR/P3P.

A site owner will need to note the following features:

- Entity
- Disclosure
- Assurances
- Data collection and purpose

Entity specifies who is responsible for the site and how a user can contact the site owner. *Disclosure* specifies where the written policy is on the site. *Assurances* tell what third party or law ensures that the site owner follows the policy. Finally, *data collection and purpose* describes which data is collected and how it is used.

It should, however, be stressed that it is a not a trivial task to translate the written policy together with the information on which policies to apply to which pages for a set of P3P policies. Therefore, a number of P3P policy generators are available. Three examples of such generators are as follows:

- IBM P3P Policy editor
- PrivacyBot.com
- P3Pedit

These tools should assist the creator of a P3P policy or policies. Before selecting one of these tools, verify that it supports the most current version of the P3P specification. In Chapter 11, a more detailed description of such tools is given.

Typically, these tools guide the user through a number of steps and ask him or her to fill in a number of fields, though there are exceptions to this approach. All fields must be filled in to receive a correct and complete policy. The output from such a tool is a set of P3P policies in the standardized XML format.

In P3P, there are currently 17 predefined data categories, including the "other" category:

- Physical
- Online
- Unique-id
- Purchase
- Financial
- Computer
- Navigation
- Interactive
- Demographic
- Content
- State
- Political
- Health
- Preference
- Location
- Government
- Other

Physical is used to specify the physical contact information. *Computer* keeps information about the computer system the individual is using to access the network. The category *location* is used to identify an individual's current physical location. All the categories are defined in version 1.0 of the P3P specification. In newer versions, additional categories might be defined, or some might have been removed. We recommend that you look at the current P3P specification for more information before using the categories.

NOTE

The W3C recommends that the "other" category should be used only when none of the other 16 classes fits. Check this carefully!

In addition, all collected data should be classified into one of the following 12 predefined purpose classes (see Chapter 9 for details):

- Current
- Admin
- Develop
- Tailoring
- Pseudo-analysis
- Pseudo-decision
- Individual analysis
- Individual decision
- Contact
- Historical
- Telemarketing
- Other-purpose

If the class *current* is used, data may be used by the service provider to complete the activity for which it was provided. The *other-purpose* category may be used in ways not captured by the other categories. This category should be used only if no other category fits.

Furthermore, there are six options to describe who has access to the data:

- Ours
- Delivery
- Same
- Other-recipient
- Unrelated
- Public

The first category implies that only the site owner plus entities acting as our agents will have access to the collected data. If the last category is used, data should be regarded as public. This may imply that data might be distributed on bulletin boards, in public directories, or in commercial CD-ROM directories.

Finally, there are five options to specify how long the data is being retained:

- No-retention
- Stated-purpose
- Legal-requirement
- Business-practices
- Indefinitely

The first category is used when personal data is stored only during an online interaction. When the interaction is completed, all data must be deleted. The category *indefinitely*, on the other hand, should always be used when there is an absence of a retention policy.

If multiple privacy policies are used for a site, they should be saved separately. If, for example, three policies are used, they should be saved as "policy1.xml," "policy2.xml," and "policy3.xml."

Step 4—Create a P3P Policy Reference File

Web browsers are informed about where to look for the P3P policy on any given page via a policy reference file. This file should be saved as p3p.xml in the server's root directory. In the same directory, all policy files should also be stored.

Hence, creating the policy reference file is the fourth step in making a Web site P3P compliant. Most P3P editors, mentioned previously, will assist in creating this reference file.

The following XML code is an example of a P3P policy reference file. The particular example was caught from the P3P 1.0 specification.

```
<META xmlns="http://www.w3.org/2001/09/P3Pv1">
   <POLICY-REFERENCES>
      <POLICY-REF about="/P3P/Policy3.xml">
         <INCLUDE>/cgi-bin/</INCLUDE>
```

```
5:             <INCLUDE>/servlet/</INCLUDE>
6:             <EXCLUDE>/sevlet/unknown</EXCLUDE>
7:         </POLICY-REF>
8:
9:          <POLICY-REF about="/P3P/Policy2.xml">
10:              <INCLUDE>/catalog/</INCLUDE>
11:          </POLICY-REF>
12:
13:          <POLICY-REF about="/P3P/Policy1.xml">
14:              <INCLUDE>/*</INCLUDE>
15:              <EXCLUDE>/sevlet/unknown</EXCLUDE>
16:          </POLICY-REF>
17:      </POLICY-REFERENCES>
18: </META>
```

In this example, we have added line numbers on the left-hand side for easier references in the following paragraph; however, they are not included in a real policy reference file.

The first line specifies that version 1 of the P3P specification is used. The XML tag `<POLICY-REFERENCES>` on line 2 tells us that this is a policy reference file. Furthermore, three different policies are used and referenced, Policy1.xml (lines 13-16), Policy2.xml (lines 9-11), and Policy3.xml (lines 3-7). Policy3 covers all files and subdirectories in the "cgi-bin" and the "servlet" subdirectories with the exception of the "servlet/unknown" subdirectory. Policy2 refers to the subdirectory "catalog", while Policy1 covers all other files and subdirectories excluding the directories covered in Policy3 and Policy2 plus the "servlet/unknown" subdirectory. In this particular example, the subdirectory "servlet/unknown" is not at all covered by any policy, and this should be noted in the human-readable privacy policy.

A more detailed description of policy reference files is given in Chapter 9.

Step 5—Validate the Policies

The last step is to validate the suggested policies. This can be done automatically by simply going to `http://www.w3.org/P3P/validator.html` and entering a URL for the site to evaluate. In case of errors, an error message will be displayed.

Any policy error should be eliminated and solved. Going back to Step 3 does this. When there are no more errors, the process is finished.

After this, you should also check the policies against one of the filtering tools (like MSIE6 or the JRC APPEL evaluator, which now has a toolkit for evaluating policies against different rule-sets). See Chapter 11 for more information on how to do this.

Summary

This chapter has been an introduction to what needs to be done to create a P3P policy. In the next chapter, we discuss what should be included in a human-readable policy. You can also look at the example given in Appendix C.

Additional Reading

At `http://www.w3.org/P3P/details.html`, you can find a guide to make your Web site P3P compliant.

CHAPTER 8

Privacy Policy in English

In this chapter, we discuss further the task of creating a written privacy policy. As mentioned in the previous chapter, the policy should be written in a natural language, such as English. Users with non–P3P-compliant user-agents should be able to read and understand a particular site's privacy policy without needing to understand P3P.

In addition, it is not possible to say everything with P3P. A machine-readable language can never express the same nuances as a natural one.

Information in an Online Privacy Policy

The online privacy policy document is essentially a promise (or an agreement) about how the site owner handles personal data. It is important first to state in that policy who owns the site, who manages the site, and to whom the user can complain if the policy is not fulfilled. It should also answer the following questions regarding the collection of personal data:

- What type of personal data is collected?
- Why is personal data collected?
- How is the collected personal data used?
- Is the collected personal data redistributed or shared with other organizations?

- How is collected personal data protected?
- How can I access my own personal data?
- Whom do I contact with questions about the privacy policy?

These questions are addressed in the following sections.

What Type of Personal Data Is Collected?

In a privacy policy, it is important to state the type of personal data that is stored. Name, email address, birth date or age, gender, home and work addresses, telephone number, and IP address are all examples of often-collected personal identifiable data.

We would like to distinguish between two different data collection approaches. In one approach, the user manually enters personal data either digitally or on paper. This may be done by asking the user to fill in a form when signing up at the site or when entering a particular part of the site. If personal data is gathered in this way, it is likely that the user understands that the data will be stored.

The other data collection approach is one that utilizes technology to collect data automatically. For instance, HTTP header information, such as IP addresses, is most often logged using this approach.

Figure 8.1 shows various types of data collection.

Within the figure are the user's preferences. These can be privacy related, but also preferences regarding which home page to start with or which bank account number to use as default.

At the bottom layer is the HTTP-related information that a Web server normally logs; see Chapter 4. Remember that this data can be mined for information, where tracing the behavior can retrieve the user's surf habits.

The second layer, Context & Device, is the device- and connection-dependent data. This is normally applicable for mobile Internet connections, where, for example, the MSISDN number for a mobile Internet connection (that is, the phone number), the device capabilities, such as browser type, name of the phone, IMSI number (a unique number specifying the device), and location can be sent with the request. We are not saying that this is always transmitted, but merely implying that this could be the case.

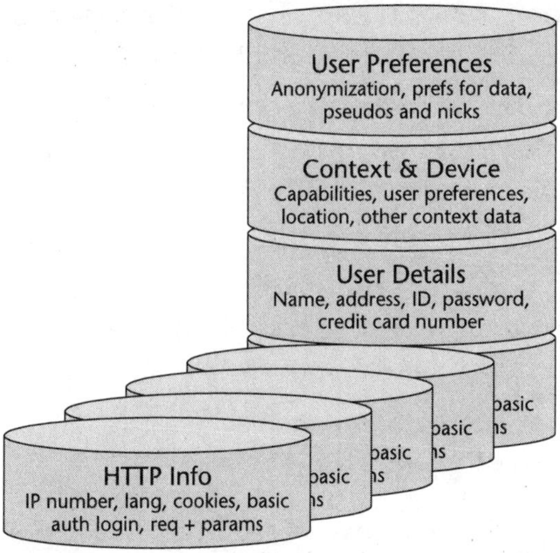

Figure 8.1 Example of user data collection.

The third layer, User Details, is data the user stored—either directly at the site by filling in a form—or prestored within the device or browser or at an intermediary server, such as the operator, ISP, or even a third party. This data could hypothetically be transmitted behind the user's back in a future scenario.

The fourth and bottom layer is the HTTP-related information that a Web server normally logs; see the previous chapters. Remember that this data can be mined for information, where tracing the behavior can retrieve the user's surfing habits.

Why Is Personal Data Collected?

When deciding which personal data to collect, we must also consider this question: "Why is personal data collected at all?" Remember from previous chapters that personal data should be collected only if it is needed to perform a certain task and if there are no other equally good means available to perform the task. One example is that there may not be a need to store the browser-type because it is sent with each request.

Hence, there must be an explicit purpose. A few examples of explicit purposes are given here.

- At an Internet bookstore, personal data, such as name and credit card information, is needed for the customer to purchase a product.
- An Internet site with a contest gathers personal data, such as name and email address, in order to send notifications on the contest result.
- IP addresses are collected in order to return information that was requested by a user, instead of using cookies.
- HTTP log files are used to protect the server from intrusions and thus the user data that may be there.

How Is the Collected Personal Data Used?

The use of personal data must also be expressed in a privacy policy, and it must be used in accordance with the purpose mentioned previously. Note that collected personal data should never be used for a purpose not explicitly mentioned in the policy document.

Examples are as follows:

- We collect data to fill your purchase order.
- We use your data to send you information about updates and special offers.
- We use your data to personalize our Web site and provide you with a better experience.
- We use your data to prefill forms, so that you do not have to type the same information every time you visit our site.

Is the Collected Personal Data Redistributed or Shared with Other Organizations?

If data is shared with other organizations, this fact must be stated clearly. In fact, if the server is located in Europe, it is normally illegal to transmit user data to other organizations if the user has not approved the transmission. If you really do wish to share data with other organizations, you can do so if all users are anonymized, or at least pseudonymized, before transmission. Please remember that there must be nothing in the transmitted data that can be tied back to a living person. One example is if you share health information records you collected with a drug company that is interested in them. If you can change your files to exclude any personal data, but include only statistics, you will not be violating any privacy principles.

A good rule is always to be very cautious about these actions. It is very difficult to be sure that not a single person can be recognized within a database. For example, you may have a file that states there is one male person, 102 years, living in Skattkärr, Sweden (a town of about 1,000 inhabitants), infected with HIV. This is obviously personal data, despite the attempt to anonymize it.

How Is Collected Personal Data Protected?

When personal data is collected, it is important to protect it from both internal and external threats. Providing adequate security mechanisms will protect you against external threats, which were described in Chapter 3. Data must be protected both during transmissions and when it is stored.

Whenever the user provides sensitive data, the transmission should be over a secure link. Normally, this means that some kind of encryption is used—for example, Secure Socket Layer (SSL). After the data is stored, it is important to keep hackers out. With an integrity checker such as Tripwire, you can monitor and verify changes to specific files in the file system.

Authentication systems or mechanisms are also an essential component when building a secure system. It does not hurt to remind the user about selecting a sufficiently difficult password (in cases when passwords are used) and not to share it with others.

The internal threat normally has to do with people working in the organization, such as employees and hired consultants. As few people as possible should have access to the data. It is also wise to educate them in computer ethics as well as computer and network security. Do not forget the system administrators because they are the most powerful users in the whole system. When people are employed or hired as consultants to work with personal data, they should be thoroughly screened. One example of an internal threat occurs when someone working in the company gives a divorce detective access to records about a person being tracked.

How Can I Access My Own Personal Data?

According to European legislation, people must be given access to their own personal data when they ask for it. This does not mean that everything needs to be accessed from the Web site, but only that someone can produce it upon a specific request. This is where the organization's contact information comes in.

However, it is a good habit to provide the user with as much information as possible within an administration interface, where the user also has the opportunity to add, change, or delete data.

Whom Do I Contact with Questions about the Privacy Policy?

State clearly whom to contact if the user has questions about the policy. You must also define whom to contact if the user feels that the privacy policy is not fulfilled by the organization. If possible, use a third-party organization for handling disputes.

Summary

You can use this chapter as a guide to creating a human-readable privacy policy, you can look at the example given in Appendix C, but you should also take a look at other policies created by larger companies.

In the next chapter, we go through in detail how to create an online policy for P3P.

CHAPTER 9

Privacy Policy Using P3P

Now we finally create the P3P policy. It will reflect the collected material as described in the previous chapters and the policy, which should have been written in a natural language. All mention of cookies is excluded in this chapter, but their coverage is handled in a separate chapter because the use of cookies is so specific that it deserves the attention.

In this chapter, we create a sample policy that we have made general enough to cover all the issues a traditional Web site needs to regard. We have deliberately left out the parts that we think you will not need. For more complete information on creating a policy, please see the P3P specification at http://www.w3.org/TR/P3P/.

Create a Reference File

The reference file is like a site map. It ties a policy file to a resource or a set of resources.

Assuming that we have a natural language policy file, we can create one or more P3P policy files. Now, there is a difference between the two policy files. When we create the natural language policy file, we can write it in such a way that it is general for the entire site. When we create the P3P policy file, we should distinguish between the kinds of data the site collects. Normally, this implies knowing where the forms are on the site. Wherever there is a form, we need a specific policy file for it. Otherwise, all resources will claim to collect all data that is ever collected.

We can assume that you have one default policy file on the server for the basic things you always do. We assume you also have two other policy files—one for the user subscription page where all the information about the user is entered and one for the page where users can perform an actual purchase.

You would then need a reference file that looks like the following:

```
<META xmlns="http://www.w3.org/2002/01/P3Pv1">
 <POLICY-REFERENCES>
  <EXPIRY max-age="86400"/>

    <POLICY-REF about="/P3P/default_policy.xml">
      <INCLUDE>/*</INCLUDE>
      <EXCLUDE>/register/index.html</EXCLUDE>
      <EXCLUDE>/purchase/index.html</EXCLUDE>
    </POLICY-REF>

    <POLICY-REF about="/P3P/register_policy.xml">
      <INCLUDE>/register/index.html</INCLUDE>
    </POLICY-REF>

    <POLICY-REF about="/P3P/purchase_policy.xml">
      <INCLUDE>/purchase/index.html</INCLUDE>
    </POLICY-REF>

 </POLICY-REFERENCES>
</META>
```

The expiry tag indicates the time that the file is valid. If you use this tag, you should set this time to at least 86400 seconds, which is equivalent to 24 hours. This value is also the default. If you want to change the reference file, perhaps because you want to start logging a new kind of data, you must first change the policy and then wait until the number of seconds indicated in the expiry tag has passed. During this time, both the new and the old reference files are valid, so you must adhere to the stricter of the two.

The expiry tag could instead contain an exact date, which is useful if you know that you are going to change your policy on a specific day. There is a danger, though, in using this feature because external circumstances might force you to change the policies earlier, such as the construction of a new page that needs a special policy. Thus, we recommend that you use the default time previously discussed instead. It is important to stick to the stated expiry time not because a P3P negotiation will take 24 hours, but because this is the time that the user-agent needs to cache the reference file. Fetching the file takes one request and one response. Probably, a reasonable expiry time is somewhere between 48 hours and a week. We think a week is reasonable. Usually you do not need more time than that to decide if a new reference file is needed.

The reference file should be stored at the so-called well-known location. This is your domain, plus `/w3c/p3p.xml`. If your site is located at www.werespectyou.com, the reference file must be stored in www.werespectyou.com/w3c/p3p.xml. The P3P user-agent will go there to look for the file.

Many larger sites, like MSN for example, have implemented P3P by now. If you want to do this the easy way without needing to type much, you can do what we call cut-and-paste engineering. You just type in the address of one of those established sites and add the extension `/w3c/p3p.xml`—for example, `www.goodexample.com/w3c/p3p.xml`. Most HTML browsers are also XML enabled and will display the reference file with colored text in a neat, easy-to-read format. Once you see the file in your browser, you can copy and save the source, change the expiry time if needed, and change the `INCLUDE` and `EXCLUDE` tags to suit your directory system. After doing this, and after creating the policy file, you move it to your `www-root/w3c/`. In Appendix A, you can learn more about XML. If you want to test the policy at its proper location before making it valid, you can add a test tag. This means that it will be disregarded by real user-agents, and you can take your time testing the XML and making sure it works before removing the test tag and thus making it valid. An example of a policy file with a `<TEST/>` tag follows.

```
<POLICIES xmlns="http://www.w3.org/2002/01/P3Pv1">
 <POLICY name="default"
     discuri="http://www.werespectyou.com/privacy/policy.html"
     xml:lang="en">
    <TEST/>
...
  </POLICY>
</POLICIES>
```

Create the Policy File

Many advanced tools are available that will help you create good-quality policy files. In this chapter, we write the XML code ourselves. You will see that it is not difficult at all.

Create the Surrounding Tags

We start with the surrounding tags. Throughout this chapter, we continue from this frame to build a policy file. Any code in bold is the added code.

```
<POLICIES xmlns="http://www.w3.org/2002/01/P3Pv1">
  <POLICY name="default"
      discuri="http://www.werespectyou.com/privacy/policy.html"
      opturi="http://www.werespectyou.com/preferences.html"
      xml:lang="en">
  </POLICY>
</POLICIES>
```

- The `POLICIES` tag contains a reference to the P3P schema, which is located at the W3C Web site. Within the `POLICY` tag, you can place all the policies of your site. In this example, however, we are using separate files for each policy. This means that the `name` attribute within the `POLICY` tag will not be used and can be set to anything.
- `discuri` indicates the path to the natural language policy. As previously mentioned, you can probably use the same natural language policy for all your P3P policies.
- `opturi` indicates the path to a site where you can request or deny that data be used for a specific purpose. At this path, you must provide information about how to do this—preferably through a form. If you have a site where the user can manage his or her profile data, you can use this site.
- The `xml:lang` attribute tells the user which language you will use in the tags where you will enter pure text, such as consequence and entity. You can read more about this in the section entitled *P3P and Multiple-Language Support* in this chapter.

Entity Information

Now that we have the frame, we should start by adding information about the company. It is the same as the information found in the natural language policy, which we described in the previous chapter.

```
<POLICIES xmlns="http://www.w3.org/2002/01/P3Pv1">
 <POLICY name="default"
     discuri="http://www.werespectyou.com/privacy/policy.html"
     opturi="http://www.werespectyou.com/preferences.html"
     xml:lang="en">
   <ENTITY>
    <DATA-GROUP>
     <DATA ref="#business.name">WeRespectYou</DATA>
     <DATA ref="#business.contact-info.postal.street">42, Web
Street</DATA>
     <DATA ref="#business.contact-info.postal.city">Gotham City</DATA>
     <DATA ref="#business.contact-info.postal.stateprov">AA</DATA>
     <DATA ref="#business.contact-info.postal.postalcode">12345</DATA>
     <DATA ref="#business.contact-info.postal.country">USA</DATA>
     <DATA ref="#business.contact-info.online.email">privacy@werespec-
tyou.com</DATA>
     <DATA ref="#business.contact-
info.telecom.telephone.intcode">1</DATA>
     <DATA ref="#business.contact-
info.telecom.telephone.loccode">555</DATA>
     <DATA ref="#business.contact-info.telecom.telephone.num-
ber">123456</DATA>
    </DATA-GROUP>
   </ENTITY>
  </POLICY>
 </POLICIES>
```

This is important information because this is where the user should turn if he or she has any complaints. Do not enter the email address or phone number of a real person because this person can leave the company and because the address is likely to be spammed at some point. Instead, provide an address that someone goes through once or twice a day. The phone number should go to an exchange, where the personnel can redirect calls that relate to privacy issues to the right person.

Access Information

A user should have the right to access data related to him or her and to change or delete the data if it is incorrect or illegally stored. The access method could vary. The simplest way is to set up a Web page where all the data is presented and changeable and where the user can access his or her information through his or her account. The problem is, of course, that the access part requires identification. If your users do not have an account at your Web site, you cannot provide them with access to their data—at least not through a Web page.

Remember, however, that a user profile is not the only personal data stored on a server. Log files, billing records, and so on should also be possible to access. It is rare, though, that anyone asks for this data, and we have never heard of a company having routines for extracting and delivering personal data from an HTTP log file or a set of billing records.

This task is not so difficult, if you think about it. A Perl script, which uses the IP number of the user or the basic authentication ID as parameters, could easily be written. It is a wise idea to store the login of the user in the log files. If there is no such data but only a regular log file, the tricky part is making sure that the user is indeed the one who holds the IP number in question and that it was the user who did the surfing, not anyone else using a public computer or a company proxy.

Handing out security audit files is not something that is generally required by users; it is therefore acceptable to not have this as a specific routine. You can provide it only to users who really insist on having it and who can prove that the IP number is indeed theirs.

```
<POLICIES xmlns="http://www.w3.org/2002/01/P3Pv1">
 <POLICY name="default"
     discuri="http://www.werespectyou.com/privacy/policy.html"
     opturi="http://www.werespectyou.com/preferences.html"
     xml:lang="en">
  </POLICY>
  <ENTITY>
   <DATA-GROUP>
    <DATA ref="#business.name">WeRespectYou</DATA>
    <DATA ref="#business.contact-info.postal.street">42, Web
Street</DATA>
    <DATA ref="#business.contact-info.postal.city">Gotham City</DATA>
    <DATA ref="#business.contact-info.postal.stateprov">AA</DATA>
    <DATA ref="#business.contact-info.postal.postalcode">12345</DATA>
    <DATA ref="#business.contact-info.postal.country">USA</DATA>
    <DATA ref="#business.contact-info.online.email">privacy@werespectyou
.com</DATA>
    <DATA ref="#business.contact-
info.telecom.telephone.intcode">1</DATA>
    <DATA ref="#business.contact-
info.telecom.telephone.loccode">555</DATA>
    <DATA ref="#business.contact-info.telecom.telephone.num-
ber">123456</DATA>
```

```
   </DATA-GROUP>
  </ENTITY>
  <ACCESS><nonident/></ACCESS>
</POLICIES>
```

The access element shown in the preceding code snippet gives the user access to his or her information. It can be one of the following:

- `<nonident/>`—If the Web site does not collect identified data.
- `<all/>`—All identified data: Access is given to all identified data.
- `<contact-and-other/>`—Identified contact information and other identified data: Access is given to identified online and physical contact information as well as to certain other identified data.
- `<ident-contact/>`—Identifiable contact information access is given to identified online and physical contact information (for example, users can access things such as a postal address).
- `<other-ident/>`—Other identified data access is given to certain other identified data (for example, users can access things such as their online account charges).
- `<none/>`—No access is provided.

Disputes

The `<Disputes>` tag allows you to tell the user where to turn if there is a disagreement about the policy and what you will do about this. If you are not part of an independent privacy organization like TRUSTe, there may not be an obvious reason for doing so.

```
<POLICIES xmlns="http://www.w3.org/2002/01/P3Pv1">
<POLICY name="default"
    discuri="http://www.werespectyou.com/privacy/policy.html"
    opturi="http://www.werespectyou.com/preferences.html"
    xml:lang="en">
 <ENTITY>
  <DATA-GROUP>
   <DATA ref="#business.name">WeRespectYou</DATA>
   <DATA ref="#business.contact-info.postal.street">42, Web Street</DATA>
   <DATA ref="#business.contact-info.postal.city">Gotham City</DATA>
   <DATA ref="#business.contact-info.postal.stateprov">AA</DATA>
   <DATA ref="#business.contact-info.postal.postalcode">12345</DATA>
   <DATA ref="#business.contact-info.postal.country">USA</DATA>
   <DATA ref="#business.contact-info.online.email">privacy@werespectyou
.com</DATA>
```

```
    <DATA ref="#business.contact-
info.telecom.telephone.intcode">1</DATA>
    <DATA ref="#business.contact-
info.telecom.telephone.loccode">555</DATA>
    <DATA ref="#business.contact-info.telecom.telephone.num-
ber">123456</DATA>
   </DATA-GROUP>
  </ENTITY>
  <ACCESS><nonident/></ACCESS>
  <DISPUTES-GROUP>
   <DISPUTES resolution-type="service"
     service="http://customerservice.werespectyou.com"
     short-description="WeRespectYou Customer Service">
    <REMEDIES><correct/></REMEDIES>
   </DISPUTES>

   <DISPUTES resolution-type="independent" service="http://www.indepen-
dentprivacyorganization.com/" short-description="Independent Privacy
Organization">
    <LONG-DESCRIPTION>If you do not receive a satisfactory response from
WeRespectYou, then please contact "Independent Privacy Organization" at
http://www.independentprivacyorganization.com/</LONG-DESCRIPTION>
     <REMEDIES>
    <correct/>
     </REMEDIES>
    </DISPUTES>
  </DISPUTES-GROUP>
  </POLICY>
</POLICIES>
```

You can set the service attribute to point to your customer service if you have such a page.

You should also point out what you will do if an error is detected, and you can choose among <correct/>, <money/>, and <law/>. We recommend that you use <correct/>, to state that if there is a mistake, you will correct it but not pay any remedies.

There is also the possibility of adding the logo of the Independent Privacy Organization. We strongly recommend that if you want to do so, you place the logo on your own site, so that there is no HTTP request going outside your own domain, for the reasons explained in the sections on Web bugs and banners in Chapter 4. You could, of course, argue that a privacy organization can handle a request for an image without logging user-related information; however, the whole idea with this privacy exercise is for us all to learn not to give away anything unnecessarily.

Table 9.1 Possible Elements within the Remedies Tag

ELEMENT	EXPLANATION
<correct/>	Errors or wrongful actions arising in connection with the privacy policy will be remedied by the service.
<money/>	If the service provider violates its privacy policy, it will pay the individual an amount specified in the human-readable privacy policy or the amount of damages.
<law/>	Remedies for breaches of the policy statement will be determined based on the law referenced in the human-readable description.

Statements

The policy that we have created so far focuses on the header information—that is, the information that is general for the entire policy. We now create statements regarding the practices around the data. There should be at least one statement, but there will probably be several, and this is where you state how you will use the data.

There is not yet a common practice as to how the data should be named—and because most P3P user-agents are merely presenting the information, it does not really matter yet. When user-agents start making decisions on the user's behalf, naming conventions will grow much more important.

```
<POLICIES xmlns="http://www.w3.org/2002/01/P3Pv1">
 <POLICY name="default"
     discuri="http://www.werespectyou.com/privacy/policy.html"
     opturi="http://www.werespectyou.com/preferences.html"
     xml:lang="en">
  <ENTITY>
   <DATA-GROUP>
    <DATA ref="#business.name">WeRespectYou</DATA>
--
   </DATA-GROUP>
  </ENTITY>
  <ACCESS><nonident/></ACCESS>
  <DISPUTES-GROUP>
--
    </DISPUTES>
  </DISPUTES-GROUP>

  <!--Use of #dynamic.miscdata-->
```

```
<STATEMENT>
 <PURPOSE><admin/><develop/></PURPOSE>
 <RECIPIENT><ours/></RECIPIENT>
 <RETENTION><stated-purpose/></RETENTION>
 <DATA-GROUP>
  <DATA ref="#dynamic.miscdata" optional="no">
   <CATEGORIES>
    <demographic/>
    <navigation/>
    <state/>
    <uniqueid/>
    <computer/>
   </CATEGORIES>
  </DATA>
 </DATA-GROUP>
</STATEMENT>

<!--Use of data elements from base schema-->
<STATEMENT>
 <PURPOSE><admin/><develop/></PURPOSE>
 <RECIPIENT><ours/></RECIPIENT>
 <RETENTION><stated-purpose/></RETENTION>
 <DATA-GROUP>
  <DATA ref="#dynamic.clickstream"/>
  <DATA ref="#dynamic.http"/>
 </DATA-GROUP>
</STATEMENT>

<!--Use of data elements from other schema-->
<STATEMENT>
 <PURPOSE><admin/><develop/></PURPOSE>
 <RECIPIENT><ours/></RECIPIENT>
 <RETENTION><stated-purpose/></RETENTION>
 <DATA-GROUP>
  <DATA
ref="#uaprof.NetworkCharacteristics.SupportedBluetoothVersion"><DATA>
  <DATA ref="#uaprof.BrowserUA.BrowserName"></DATA>
 </DATA-GROUP>
</STATEMENT>
</POLICY>
</POLICIES>
```

The DATA-GROUP

The P3P specification mentions three ways of naming data:

- Use the dynamic.miscdata element and the appropriate categories for general descriptions.

- Use the data elements defined in the base data schema for specific descriptions.
- Use data elements defined in new data schemas for specific descriptions.

Use of dynamic.miscdata

Use of dynamic.miscdata is recommended if you have a big site and if you do not know exactly what data is collected where. It will allow you to create a general policy, categorize the data, and set up a purpose, recipient, and retention policy for each group of categories. This may sound a bit confusing—let's try an example.

At your huge Web site, you collect names, addresses, interests, and all sorts of data in different forms by using cookies and processing surf patterns. When you interview the various groups of people that perform this data collection, you do not ask them about the exact kinds of data—name, address, phone number—that they use, but rather about the categories of data that they use.

A statement after interviewing the programmers may appear like this:

```
<STATEMENT>
  <CONSEQUENCE>
In order to create efficient Web execution and to ensure that there are
no abuses to our system, we collect administrative information such as
patterns of navigation through our domain and the locale from which you
are accessing our site as identified by postal codes in order to provide
you with faster service. A small file called a "cookie" is used to main-
tain your session.
  </CONSEQUENCE>
  <PURPOSE>
    <admin/>
  </PURPOSE>
  <RECIPIENT>
    <ours/><same/>
  </RECIPIENT>
  <RETENTION>
    <business-practices/>
  </RETENTION>
  <DATA-GROUP>
    <DATA ref="#dynamic.miscdata">
    <CATEGORIES>
      <demographic/><navigation/><state/><uniqueid/><computer/>
     </CATEGORIES>
    </DATA>
  </DATA-GROUP>
</STATEMENT>
```

As you can see, the DATA tag contains a reference named dynamic.miscdata, and the information type is in the categories (see Table 9.2).

Table 9.2 Possible Elements within the Categories Tag

ELEMENT	EXPLANATION
<physical/>	**Physical contact information:** Information that allows an individual to be contacted or located in the physical world—such as telephone number or address.
<online/>	**Online contact information:** Information that allows an individual to be contacted or located on the Internet—such as email. Often, this information is independent of the specific computer used to access the network. (See the category "Computer information.")
<uniqueid/>	**Unique identifiers:** Nonfinancial identifiers, excluding government-issued identifiers, issued for purposes of consistently identifying or recognizing the individual. These include identifiers issued by a Web site or service.
<purchase/>	**Purchase information:** Information actively generated by the purchase of a product or service, including information about the method of payment.
<financial/>	**Financial information:** Information about an individual's finances including account status and activity information such as account balance, payment or overdraft history, and information about an individual's purchase or use of financial instruments including credit or debit card information. Information about a discrete purchase by an individual, as described in "Purchase information," alone does not come under the definition of "Financial information."
<computer/>	**Computer information:** Information about the computer system that the individual is using to access the network—such as the IP number, domain name, browser type, or operating system.
<navigation/>	**Navigation and clickstream data:** Data passively generated by browsing the Web site—such as which pages are visited and how long users stay on each page.
<interactive/>	**Interactive data:** Data actively generated from or reflecting explicit interactions with a service provider through its site—such as queries to a search engine or logs of account activity.

Table 9.2 *(continued)*

ELEMENT	EXPLANATION
`<demographic/>`	**Demographic and socioeconomic data:** Data about an individual's characteristics—such as gender, age, and income.
`<content/>`	**Content:** The words and expressions contained in the body of a communication—such as the text of email, bulletin board postings, or chat room communications.
`<state/>`	**State Management Mechanisms:** Mechanisms for maintaining a stateful session with a user or automatically recognizing users who have visited a particular site or accessed particular content previously—such as HTTP cookies.
`<political/>`	**Political information:** Membership in or affiliation with groups such as religious organizations, trade unions, professional associations, political parties, etc.
`<health/>`	**Health information:** Information about an individual's physical or mental health, sexual orientation, use or inquiry into health care services or products, and purchase of health care services or products.
`<preference/>`	**Preference data:** Data about an individual's likes and dislikes—such as favorite color or musical tastes.
`<location/>`	**Location data:** Information that can be used to identify an individual's current physical location and track that person as his or her location changes—such as GPS position data.
`<government/>`	**Government-issued identifiers:** Identifiers issued by a government for purposes of consistently identifying the individual.
`<other-category>` string `</other-category>`	**Other:** Other types of data not captured by the preceding definitions. (A human-readable explanation should be provided in these instances, between the `<other-category>` and the `</other-category>` tags.)

Use of Data Elements from Base Schema

The P3P protocol provides an extensive data schema; see Appendix A, "An XML Tutorial," which is located at http://www.w3.org/TR/P3P/base.

Table 9.3 shows a list of all the elements available in P3P 1.0.

Table. 9.3 The P3P Base Data Schema Definition

DATA ELEMENT	COMMENT	BELONGS TO	CATEGORY
"date" Data Structure			
date.ymd.year	Year		
date.ymd.month	Month		
date.ymd.day	Day		
date.hms.hour	Hour		
date.hms.minute	Minutes		
date.hms.second	Second		
date.fractionsecond	Fraction of second		
date.timezone	Time zone		
"login" Data Structure			
login.id	Login ID		<uniqueid/>
login.password	Login password		<uniqueid/>
"personname" Data Structure			
personname.prefix	Name prefix		<demographic/>
personname.given	Given name (first name)		<physical/>
personname.middle	Middle name		<physical/>
personname.family	Family name (last name)		<physical/>
personname.suffix	Name suffix		<demographic/>
personname.nickname	Nickname		<demographic/>
"certificate" Data Structure			
certificate.key	Certificate key		<uniqueid/>
certificate.format	Certificate format		<uniqueid/>
"telephonenum" Data Structure			
telephonenum.intcode	International telephone code		<physical/>
telephonenum.loccode	Local telephone area code		<physical/>
telephonenum.number	Telephone number		<physical/>
telephonenum.ext	Telephone extension		<physical/>

Table. 9.3 *(Continued)*

DATA ELEMENT	COMMENT	BELONGS TO	CATEGORY
telephonenum.comment	Telephone optional comments		<physical/>
"postal" Data Structure			
postal.name		#personname	
postal.street	Street address		<physical/>
postal.city	City		<demographic/>
postal.stateprov	State or province		<demographic/>
postal.postalcode	Postal code		<demographic/>
postal.organization	Organization name		<demographic/>
postal.country	Country name		<demographic/>
"telecom" Data Structure			
telecom.telephone	Telephone number	#telephonenum	<physical/>
telecom.fax	Fax number	#telephonenum	<physical/>
telecom.mobile	Mobile telephone number	#telephonenum	<physical/>
telecom.pager	Pager number	#telephonenum	<physical/>
"online" Data Structure			
online.email	Email address		<online/>
online.uri	Home page address		<online/>
"contact" Data Structure			
contact.postal	Postal address information	#postal	
contact.telecom	Telecom-munications information	#telecom	<physical/>
contact.online	Online address information	#online	<online/>
"uri" Data Structure			
uri.authority	URI authority		
uri.stem	URI stem		
uri.querystring	Query-string portion of URI		

(continues)

Table. 9.3 The P3P Base Data Schema Definition *(Continued)*

DATA ELEMENT	COMMENT	BELONGS TO	CATEGORY
"ipaddr" Data Structure			
ipaddr.hostname	Complete host and domain name		<computer/>
ipaddr.partial hostname	Partial hostname		<demographic/>
ipaddr.fullip	Full IP address		<computer/>
ipaddr.partialip	Partial IP address		<demographic/>
"loginfo" Data Structure			
loginfo.uri	URI of requested resource	#uri	<navigation/>
loginfo.timestamp	Request timestamp	#date	<navigation/>
loginfo.clientip	Client's IP address or hostname	#ipaddr	
loginfo.other .httpmethod	HTTP request method		<navigation/>
loginfo.other.bytes	Data bytes in response		<navigation/>
loginfo.other .statuscode	Response status code		<navigation/>
"httpinfo" Data Structure			
httpinfo.referer	Last URI requested by the user	#uri	<navigation/>
httpinfo.useragent	User-agent information		<computer/>
"dynamic" Data Schema			
dynamic.clickstream	Clickstream information	#loginfo	<navigation/> <computer/> <demographic/>
dynamic.http	HTTP protocol information	#httpinfo	<navigation/> <computer/>
dynamic.clientevents	User's interaction with a resource		<navigation/>
dynamic.cookies	Use of HTTP cookies		

Table. 9.3 *(Continued)*

DATA ELEMENT	COMMENT	BELONGS TO	CATEGORY
`dynamic.searchtext`	Search terms		<interactive/>
`dynamic.interaction record`	Server stores the transaction history		<interactive/>
`dynamic.miscdata`	Miscellaneous nonbase data schema		
"user" Data Schema			
`user.name`	User's name	#personname	<physical/> <demographic/>
`user.bdate`	User's birth date	#date	<demographic/>
`user.login`	User's login information	#login	<uniqueid/>
`user.cert`	User's identity certificate	#certificate	<uniqueid/>
`user.gender`	User's gender		<demographic/>
`user.jobtitle`	User's job title		<demographic/>
`user.home-info`	User's home contact information	#contact	<physical/> <online/> <demographic/>
`user.business-info`	User's business contact information	#contact	<physical/> <online/> <demographic/>
`user.employer`	Name of user's employer		<demographic/>
`user.department`	Department or division of organization where user is employed		<demographic/>
"thirdparty" Data Schema			
`thirdparty.name`	Third party's name	#personname	<physical/> <demographic/>
`thirdparty.bdate`	Third party's birth date	#date	<demographic/>
`thirdparty.login`	Third party's login information	#login	<uniqueid/>
`thirdparty.cert`	Third party's identity certificate	#certificate	<uniqueid/>

(continues)

Table. 9.3 The P3P Base Data Schema Definition *(Continued)*

DATA ELEMENT	COMMENT	BELONGS TO	CATEGORY
`thirdparty.gender`	Third party's gender		<demographic/>
`thirdparty.jobtitle`	Third party's job title		<demographic/>
`thirdparty.home-info`	Third party's home contact information	#contact	<physical/> <online/> <demographic/>
`thirdparty.business-info`	Third party's business contact information	#contact	<physical/> <online/> <demographic/>
`thirdparty.employer`	Name of third party's employer		<demographic/>
`thirdparty.department`	Department or division of organization where third party is employed		<demographic/>
"business" Data Schema			
`business.name`	Organization name		<demographic/>
`business.department`	Department or division of organization		<demographic/>
`business.cert`	Organization identity certificate	#certificate	<uniqueid/>
`business.contact-info`	Contact information for the organization	#contact	<physical/> <online/> <demographic/>

As you can see, you can choose from a wide range of data elements from the base schema. The first column shows the name of the data structure. The second gives a short description. The third is used if the data structure itself contains a structure.

For example, the user's postal information is denoted as user.home-info.postal. If you look up user information, you can see that user.home-info is a contact structure and that it contains an element named contact.postal. You can be even more specific. The user's office phone number is denoted as user.business-info.telecom.telephone. user.business-info is a contact. contact.telecom is a telecom. telecom contains telephone.

In the fourth column, you can see what category the information belongs to, if you decide to use the dynamic.miscdata instead, as in the previous section.

Use of Data Elements from Other Schema

Even though there are so many elements to choose from, there may be a need for more. For example, we found it necessary to define a schema for WAP 1.2.1 user-agents, and in 2001, together with two colleagues, we developed one. If you do use a schema that is not formally accepted, you should remember that it takes a compliant user-agent to understand it.

The CONSEQUENCE Tag

Now that we have found a way to describe the data that is collected, we can add a consequence tag to the statement. The consequence contains human-readable information about what you are about to do to the data in the statement, why, and for how long.

The tag is optional, but it will most likely be shown by a viewer, which we discuss in Chapter 11. It will probably also be displayed to the user by a user-agent that finds a mismatch between the user's privacy preferences and the policy—for example, "The site collects your home telephone number. OK to retrieve?" may display where the statement reports to the user that this data collection will be a consequence of using the site.

The NONIDENTIFIABLE Tag

If your site collects data that cannot be tied back to a user, you can clarify this in a statement containing a nonidentifiable tag. In this case it must be nearly impossible to tie identifiable data back to a user. For example, a logged IP number is not acceptable as nonidentifiable data. You can use this tag to say that you do not collect any data or that you anonymize or pseudonymize data upon collection, then add a datagroup containing all the categories that you collect.

The anonymization or pseudonymization must be nonreversible. How the information is anonymized or pseudonymized must be explained in the natural-language privacy policy.

If you use the nonidentifiable tag, the purpose, recipient, and retention tags described in the following sections are not necessary.

The PURPOSE Tag

There are 11 predefined purposes of data collection that you can choose from—thus, the lifeline that is the twelfth tag, `<other-purpose/>`, should not have to be used.

Table 9.4 shows the descriptions as described in the P3P specification.

Table 9.4 Possible Elements within the Purpose Tag

ELEMENT	EXPLANATION
`<current/>`	**Completion and support of activity for which data was provided**: Information may be used by the service provider to complete the activity for which it was provided, whether it is a one-time activity (such as returning the results from a Web search, forwarding an email message, or placing an order) or a recurring activity (such as providing a subscription service or allowing access to an online address book or electronic wallet).
`<admin/>`	**Web site and system administration**: Information may be used for the technical support of the Web site and its computer system. This would include processing computer account information, information used in the course of securing and maintaining the site, and verification of Web site activity by the site or its agents.
`<develop/>`	**Research and development**: Information may be used to enhance, evaluate, or otherwise review the site, service, product, or market. This does not include personal information used to tailor or modify the content to the specific individual or information used to evaluate, target, profile, or contact the individual.
`<tailoring/>`	**One-time tailoring**: Information may be used to tailor or modify content or design of the site where the information is used only for a single visit to the site and not used for any kind of future customization. For example, an online store might suggest other items a visitor may wish to purchase based on the items he or she has already placed in his or her shopping basket.

Table 9.4 *(Continued)*

ELEMENT	EXPLANATION
`<pseudo-analysis/>`	**Pseudonymous analysis**: Information may be used to create or build a record of a particular individual or computer that is tied to a pseudonymous identifier, without tying identified data (such as name, address, phone number, or email address) to the record. This profile will be used to determine the habits, interests, or other characteristics of individuals for the purpose of research, analysis, and reporting, but it will not be used to attempt to identify specific individuals. For example, a marketer may wish to understand the interests of visitors to different portions of a Web site.
`<pseudo-decision/>`	**Pseudonymous decision**: Information may be used to create or build a record of a particular individual or computer that is tied to a pseudonymous identifier, without tying identified data (such as name, address, phone number, or email address) to the record. This profile will be used to determine the habits, interests, or other characteristics of individuals to make a decision that directly affects that individual, but it will not be used to attempt to identify specific individuals. For example, a marketer may tailor or modify content displayed to the browser based on pages viewed during previous visits.
`<individual-analysis/>`	**Individual analysis**: Information may be used to determine the habits, interests, or other characteristics of individuals and combine it with identified data for the purpose of research, analysis, and reporting. For example, an online Web site for a physical store may wish to analyze how online shoppers make offline purchases.
`<individual-decision/>`	**Individual decision**: Information may be used to determine the habits, interests, or other characteristics of individuals and combine it with identified data to make a decision that directly affects that individual. For example, an online store suggests items a visitor may wish to purchase based on items he or she has purchased during previous visits to the Web site.
`<contact/>`	**Contacting visitors for marketing of services or products**: Information may be used to contact the individual, through a communications channel other than voice telephone, for the promotion of a product or service. This includes notifying visitors about updates to the Web site. This does not include a direct reply to a question or comment or customer service for a single transaction—in those cases, `<current/>`

(continues)

Table 9.4 Possible Elements within the Purpose Tag *(Continued)*

ELEMENT	EXPLANATION
<contact/> *(continued)*	would be used. In addition, this does not include marketing via customized Web content or banner advertisements embedded in sites the user is visiting—these cases would be covered by the <tailoring/>, <pseudo-analysis/> and <pseudo-decision/>, or <individual-analysis/> and <individual-decision/> purposes.
`<historical/>`	**Historical preservation**: Information may be archived or stored for the purpose of preserving social history as governed by an existing law or policy. This law or policy MUST be referenced in the `<DISPUTES>` element and MUST include a specific definition of the type of qualified researcher who can access the information, where this information will be stored, and specifically how this collection advances the preservation of history.
`<telemarketing/>`	**Contacting visitors for marketing of services or products via telephone**: Information may be used to contact the individual via a voice telephone call for promotion of a product or service. This does not include a direct reply to a question or comment or customer service for a single transaction—in those cases, `<current/>` would be used.
`<other-purpose> enter description within the tag </other-purpose>`	**Other uses**: Information may be used in other ways not captured by the previous definitions. (A human-readable explanation MUST be provided in these instances.)

Nonscientific research has shown that the `<admin/>` and `<current/>` tags appear to be preferred by those who published P3P policies until now.

If you are providing the user with the possibility to opt in or opt out of data collection, you can add a `required` attribute to all the preceding tags except the `<current/>` tag. The `required` attribute shows whether it is possible to opt in or opt out of data collection—that is, if it is possible to choose whether the data element is to be collected. The `required` attribute has three values:

- *always*, if data collection always takes place. This is usually the default.

- *opt-in*, whether the user explicitly asks for the data collection—for example, if the user has selected the collection himself or herself.
- *opt-out*, if the user has to make an active choice not to have the data collected.

If you say there is a possibility to opt in or opt out, you must specify an `opturi`, as previously discussed in the *Create the Surrounding Tags* section of this chapter, so that the user can change his or her preferences.

As an example, let's say that you have a site where you require the user to state his or her gender in order to have an account. On the same site, the user can choose to give away information about his or her phone number. Also, the user's IP address and/or cookies are used for other purposes than administrative, and this collection will have to be actively refused for it not to take place.

This would then give the following statements:

```
<STATEMENT>
 <PURPOSE><current/><individual-analysis required="always"/></PURPOSE>
 <RECIPIENT><ours/></RECIPIENT>
 <RETENTION><stated-purpose/></RETENTION>
 <DATA-GROUP>
  <DATA ref="#user.gender"/>
 </DATA-GROUP>
</STATEMENT>

<STATEMENT>
 <PURPOSE><current/><individual-analysis required="opt-in"/></PURPOSE>
 <RECIPIENT><ours/></RECIPIENT>
 <RETENTION><stated-purpose/></RETENTION>
 <DATA-GROUP>
  <DATA ref="#user.home-info.telecom.telephone"/>
 </DATA-GROUP>
</STATEMENT>

<STATEMENT>
 <PURPOSE><current/><individual-analysis required="opt-out"/></PUR-
POSE>
 <RECIPIENT><ours/></RECIPIENT>
 <RETENTION><stated-purpose/></RETENTION>
 <DATA-GROUP>
  <DATA ref="#loginfo.clientip.fullip"/>
  <DATA ref="#dynamic.cookies"/>
 </DATA-GROUP>
</STATEMENT>
```

After stating the purpose of the data collection, you will now have to say only with whom you will share it and for how long.

The RECIPIENT Tag

Something most users are interested in is whether you are planning to share their data with other parties. You will have to state all the receivers of the information; how the information is transmitted does not matter. For example, if you have banners at your site, and if you provide the advertisers with information about the user through parameters to the image (see Chapter 4), this should be stated here.

All the tags can either be stand-alone or contain a <recipient-description> tag, where a description of the recipient is stated. A required attribute can also be added to all the recipient tags, except <ours/>, just as with purpose tags; see the previous section.

Table 9.5 shows all the allowed tags, as described in the P3P specification.

Assume that you share the user's gender information with your advertiser, by passing it through the banner tag as described in Chapter 3:

```
<img src="http://advertiser.com/banner.gif?usergender=F">
```

You would then have to indicate this by adding a statement as shown here:

```
<STATEMENT>
 <PURPOSE><current/><pseudo-analysis/></PURPOSE>
 <RECIPIENT><unrelated/></RECIPIENT>
 <RETENTION><stated-purpose/></RETENTION>
 <DATA-GROUP>
  <DATA ref="#user.gender"/>
 </DATA-GROUP>
</STATEMENT>
```

You can also describe the recipient as shown in this statement:

```
<STATEMENT>
 <PURPOSE><current/><pseudo-analysis/></PURPOSE>
 <RECIPIENT>
   <unrelated>
     <recipient-description>
We share information about your gender with our advertisers. The information is not in itself personally identifiable, unless the advertiser can identify the user through the IP number or through the use of a small file called a cookie.
     </recipient-description>
   </unrelated>
```

```
  </RECIPIENT>
  <RETENTION><stated-purpose/></RETENTION>
  <DATA-GROUP>
   <DATA ref="#user.gender"/>
  </DATA-GROUP>
</STATEMENT>
```

Table 9.5 Possible Elements within the Recipient Tag

ELEMENT	EXPLANATION
`<ours>`	**Ourselves and/or entities acting as our agents or entities for whom we are acting as an agent**: An agent in this instance is defined as a third party that processes data only on behalf of the service provider for the completion of the stated purposes. (For example, the service provider and its printing bureau prints address labels and does nothing further with the information.)
`<delivery>`	**Delivery services possibly following different practices**: Legal entities performing delivery services that may use data for purposes other than completion of the stated purpose. This should also be used for delivery services whose data practices are unknown.
`<same>`	**Legal entities following our practices**: Legal entities that use the data on their own behalf under equable practices. (For example, consider a service provider that grants the user access to collected personal information and also provides it to a partner who uses it once but discards it. Because the recipient, who has otherwise similar practices, cannot grant the user access to information that it discarded, they are considered to have equable practices.)
`<other-recipient>`	**Legal entities following different practices**: Legal entities that are constrained by and accountable to the original service provider, but may use the data in a way not specified in the service provider's practices. (For example, the service provider collects data that is shared with a partner who may use it for other purposes. It is in the service provider's interest to ensure that the data is not used in a way that would be considered abusive to the users' and its own interests.)
`<unrelated>`	**Unrelated third parties**: Legal entities whose data usage practices are not known by the original service provider.
`<public>`	**Public forums**: Public forums such as bulletin boards, public directories, or commercial CD-ROM directories.

The RETENTION Tag

Retention is actually about retaining data and how often you clean up your log files or customer databases. This tag, however, does not make you promise "six weeks" for a Web server log file or "two years" for a customer database.

Table 9.6 shows a list of the possible tags as described in the P3P specification.

Table 9.6 Possible Elements within the Retention Tag

ELEMENT	EXPLANATION
`<no-retention/>`	**Information is not retained** for more than the brief period of time necessary to make use of it during the course of a single online interaction. Information MUST be destroyed following this interaction and MUST NOT be logged, archived, or otherwise stored. This type of retention policy would apply, for example, to services that do not keep Web server logs, set cookies only for use during a single session, or collect information to perform a search but do not keep logs of searches performed.
`<stated-purpose/>`	**For the stated purpose:** Information is retained to meet the stated purpose. This requires that information be discarded as soon as possible. Sites MUST have a retention policy that establishes a destruction timetable. The retention policy MUST be included in or linked from the site's human-readable privacy policy.
`<legal-requirement/>`	**As required by law or liability under applicable law:** Information is retained to meet a stated purpose, but the retention period is longer because of a legal requirement or liability. For example, a law may allow consumers to dispute transactions for a certain time period; therefore, a business may for liability reasons decide to maintain records of transactions, or a law may affirmatively require a certain business to maintain records for auditing or other soundness purposes. Sites MUST have a retention policy that establishes a destruction timetable. The retention policy MUST be included in or linked from the site's human-readable privacy policy.

Table 9.6 *(Continued)*

ELEMENT	EXPLANATION
`<business-practices/>`	**Determined by service provider's business practice:** Information is retained under a service provider's stated business practices. Sites MUST have a retention policy that establishes a destruction timetable. The retention policy MUST be included in or linked from the site's human-readable privacy policy.
`<indefinitely/>`	**Indefinitely**: Information is retained for an indeterminate period of time. The absence of a retention policy would be reflected under this option. Where the recipient is a public forum, this is the appropriate retention policy.

After having added the retention tag, the statement is complete, and so is the policy.

It is now ready to be tested through a P3P validator, which we discuss in Chapter 11.

P3P and Multiple-Language Support

If your server is located in a non–English-speaking country, you may want to show the natural-language tags in the policy, such as `<CONSEQUENCE>`, `<other-purpose>`, `<LONG-DESCRIPTION>`, and `<recipient-description>`, in different languages, depending on the user's preferred language.

In that case, you may choose to create several policies or to generate a policy where the natural-language tags are placed in the policy upon delivery. In order to find the appropriate language, you can use the `accept-language` HTTP header field in the request for the policy. A P3P user-agent might not deliver this information while negotiating.

If you wish to support only one language, or if you have determined that the user wants a particular language from the request header, you can add this information through the `content-language` HTTP response header.

If there is no information about the preferred language of the user, and if you do want to provide the user with natural-language tags according to his or her preferences, you can choose to send several policies with the response and let the user-agent select which one to use. There are several tags where you can add this information. We recommend that you use it in the policy tag. By doing this, you can give the user-agent several policies inside a <POLICIES> tag:

```
<POLICIES xmlns="http://www.w3.org/2002/01/P3Pv1">
 <POLICY name="default"
      discuri="http://www.werespectyou.com/privacy/policy_en.html"
      xml:lang="en">
...
  </POLICY>
<POLICY name="default"
      discuri="http://www.werespectyou.com/privacy/policy_de.html"
      xml:lang="i-klingon">
...
  </POLICY>
</POLICIES>
```

As a result, the user-agent does not give away more information than needed during the agreement, according to the safe-zone principle; on the other hand, you will have to send more information than needed to make sure that what the user receives corresponds to what he or she needs. This is not so good if the receiver is a mobile device and the transmission takes place over the air.

Our recommendation is not to overdo the language presentation, unless your business is located in a country where Web users do not understand English; however, you still need a policy in English because some users are from abroad.

For example, if your entire site is in Finnish, there is hardly a need to present the natural-language tags in English. If your site is in both English and Finnish, it is probably enough to present the policy in English because most Fins speak English very well. If your site is in Spain and the content is presented in both Spanish and English, you may wish to present the policy in both Spanish and English. There is probably no need, though, to add a Catalan policy because Catalan-speaking surfers will understand either English or Spanish. Then again, the Catalan-speaking surfers may not agree with this, at least not the ones we know.

Still, try to keep it simple, and remember that the real natural-language presentation is in the full policy—you can have as many of those as you wish.

The Legal Perspective on Policies

Let's assume for a minute that you collect email addresses at your site and then sell them to spammers. We do not need to argue again that this is unethical and will turn all your customers against you. The assumption is only hypothetical reasoning.

Assume you create a statement in your policy that looks like this:

```
<STATEMENT>
 <PURPOSE><contact/></PURPOSE>
 <RECIPIENT><public/></RECIPIENT>
 <RETENTION><indefinitely/></RETENTION>
 <DATA-GROUP>
  <DATA ref="#user.business-info.online.email"/>
  <DATA ref="#user.home-info.online.email"/>
 </DATA-GROUP>
</STATEMENT>
```

Let's also assume that you create a natural-language policy that says the same thing: "We will use this information to contact you, we will share it with anyone, and you cannot count on our removing it."

In countries with strong privacy legislation, such as the European Union Member States, which include Sweden, Belgium, and France, this policy is still not enough. The only thing that can allow this action to take place is for the user to explicitly give his or her consent to it.

In a country that does not have strong data protection laws, the policy will probably count as a legal contract. On the other hand, it could be argued that the policy does not do much good. If there is a P3P user-agent acting on it, you are not likely to get past it anyway.

If you plan to say "I'm going to be really bad," you might as well not say it at all. Assume that you state that you will do the right thing, as in the following policy:

```
<STATEMENT>
 <PURPOSE><current/></PURPOSE>
 <RECIPIENT><ours/></RECIPIENT>
 <RETENTION><stated-purpose/></RETENTION>
```

```
<DATA-GROUP>
  <DATA ref="#user.business-info.online.email"/>
  <DATA ref="#user.home-info.online.email"/>
</DATA-GROUP>
</STATEMENT>
```

If you do not adhere to this statement, then you might be sued for breaking a contract.

The most important thing is that the policy will not be blocked byP3P user-agents. You will have to follow both the policy and the law of the country where your business is located.

Summary

In this chapter, we have thoroughly described all the steps necessary to create a P3P policy. We have not discussed all the possible alternatives, though; you may want to read the specification for details.

In the next chapter, we explain how P3P handles cookies.

Additional Reading

http://www.w3.org/P3P	The P3P site
http://www.w3.org/TR/P3P	The P3P specification
http://www.ietf.org/rfc/rfc1766.txt	Tags for the identification of languages

CHAPTER 10

Cookies and P3P

We have already discussed cookies and the harm they can do in Chapter 4 and Chapter 6. We have also discussed when and why they are useful. P3P handles cookies in two ways. One is through regular policies, and the other is through compact policies.

Cookies Revisited

There are four kinds of cookies:

- Session cookies live only through the session.
- Persistent cookies remain even after the session is closed.
- First-party cookies belong to the site where you chose to go.
- Third-party cookies are fetched from a site whose content is retrieved indirectly, normally through an image tag.

NOTE

Keep in mind that the technical distinction between first- and third-party cookies rules the cookie filtering and preference tools, not the legal distinction.

We have already discussed how cookies are sent with the request that fetches the requested page and set with the response that comes back.

If no cookie is stored at the user's side, an HTTP request might look like the one shown in Listing 10.1:

```
GET /index.php HTTP/1.1
HOST: www.werespectyou.com
```

Listing 10.1 A simple HTTP request.

We also learned that cookies are set in the response header, which accompanies the requested site, shown in Listing 10.2:

```
HTTP/1.1 200 OK
Date: Sat, 26 Jan 2002 21:39:26 GMT
Server: Apache/1.3.20 (Win32)
X-Powered-By: PHP/4.0.6
Connection: close
Content-Type: text/html
Set-Cookie: test_cookie=105619988554242950293147325001629502929;
Comment=CheckForPermission
```

Listing 10.2 An HTTP response containing a set-cookie.

The response header will set a cookie with the content shown in Listing 10.3, assuming this is fine with the user—that is, assuming it is not filtered away:

```
test_cookie
CheckForPermission
werespectyou.com/
105619988554242950293147325001629502929*
```

Listing 10.3 The stored information.

The next time the Web site is accessed by this user, or through this computer, the cookie will be sent by the browser within the request header as shown in Listing 10.4:

```
GET /index.php HTTP/1.1
HOST: www.werespectyou.com
Cookie: test_cookie=10561998855424295029314732500162950929
```

Listing 10.4 The next HTTP request containing the cookie.

All the preceding actions are normally transparent to the user.

Normally, as a developer, you will not set a cookie if you get one. You will note only that this is the user Greta coming back to your site, and because you already know her, this is how you react to her request.

P3P and Cookies

With Internet Explorer 6 (IE6) and Netscape 7, a new generation of cookie filtering tools appeared. They use a mix of user preferences, with default settings for those who do not bother about privacy, and they use P3P handshaking to decide which cookies to accept or reject. This came as a surprise to many third-party cookie setters out there on the Internet, who suddenly discovered that their cookies were blocked.

Cookie Filtering

Almost as long as there have been cookies, there have been cookie filtering tools. They were developed to block, warn, or allow cookies, depending on the type of cookie or the site that was trying to set it. They usually handle the user preferences by asking once and then use a remember-this-decision mechanism.

Because most people were very happy not knowing what cookies did to them, most people never heard about cookie filtering tools. Cookie filtering tools, as well as other privacy tools like webwashers, were generally used by privacy-aware computer nerds. Since 2000 or 2001, however, the public has increased its interest in privacy, probably because spam has raised people's awareness, and the legislators in some countries decided that all users need protection, not only those who can look after themselves.

Internet Explorer 6 and Netscape 7 use the following default privacy setting:

- First-party cookies are allowed.
- Third-party cookies are allowed if they have a policy *unless* the policy says they collect personal information without your consent.

You can then alter the filtering preferences and set the browser to allow, prompt, or reject cookies based on other information, such as whether the P3P policy says it will collect information only with your implicit consent or without your explicit consent, or whether the cookies are session, persistent, and a mix of both. You can also, in both browsers, decide to remove all cookies set by a site at the end of the session, while "cheating" all the parties out there that allowed you to do things at their Web sites, thinking that they had stored a persistent cookie on your computer.

That idea is not dumb at all, we think.

Full Policies

Maybe you are reading this book to find out how to get your cookies past the IE6 filter easily. In that case, you will probably choose to create only a compact policy. We start, though, by describing a full P3P agreement.

We already learned that a regular P3P agreement normally requires three HTTP requests, which we have illustrated in Figure 10.1. One request gets the reference file, one gets the policy file, and the last one retrieves the required site.

We now go back to the policy file we created in Chapter 9, but we focus our attention only on how to include cookies.

Create a Reference File

If cookies are included in the policy that is referred to by the <POLICY-REF> element, then you can simply add a <COOKIE-INCLUDE/> element as shown in the code that follows. If you have different policies for different cookies, you can specify them by adding their names, values, domains, and paths. You can also describe the exact sites, or set of sites, that will set the cookies.

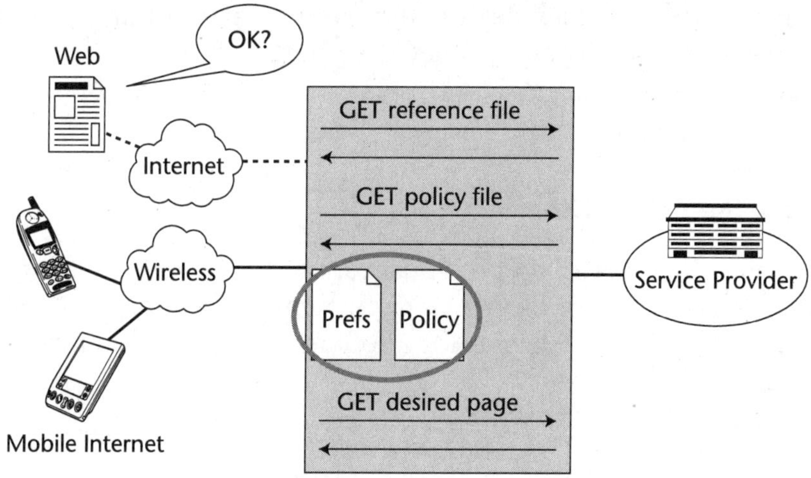

Figure 10.1 A full P3P agreement.

```
<META xmlns="http://www.w3.org/2002/01/P3Pv1">
 <POLICY-REFERENCES>
  <EXPIRY max-age="86400"/>

    <POLICY-REF about="/P3P/default_policy.xml">
      <INCLUDE>/*</INCLUDE>
      <EXCLUDE>/register/index.html</EXCLUDE>
      <EXCLUDE>/purchase/index.html</EXCLUDE>
    </POLICY-REF>

    <POLICY-REF about="/P3P/register_policy.xml">
      <INCLUDE>/register/index.html</INCLUDE>
      <COOKIE-INCLUDE/>
    </POLICY-REF>

    <POLICY-REF about="/P3P/purchase_policy.xml">
      <INCLUDE>/purchase/index.html</INCLUDE>
    </POLICY-REF>

    <POLICY-REF about="/P3P/cookie_policy.xml">
      <COOKIE-INCLUDE>/info/*</COOKIE-INCLUDE>
    </POLICY-REF>

 </POLICY-REFERENCES>
</META>
```

The example indicates that all the cookies set by the /register/ index.html page will be described in the register_policy.xml policy file, wheras all the cookies set by the /info/* part of the site will be described by the cookie_policy.xml policy file. Just as with the <EXCLUDE> element, you can also use <COOKIE-EXCLUDE>. We, however, will keep this simple.

Create the Policy File

The policy files described previously should have a statement that contains a #dynamic.cookies data element, indicating that the policy statement applies to the use of the cookies set by the resource:

```
<STATEMENT>
 <PURPOSE><current/><individual-analysis/></PURPOSE>
 <RECIPIENT><ours/></RECIPIENT>
 <RETENTION><stated-purpose/></RETENTION>
 <DATA-GROUP>
  <DATA ref="#dynamic.cookies"/>
 </DATA-GROUP>
</STATEMENT>
```

Within this statement, the purpose, recipient, and retention policy for the cookie are described. Except for the presence of this element, the policy should look the same as in Chapter 9.

Compact Policies

A compact policy is an abbreviated version of a full policy—a sort of quick and dirty way to perform a P3P agreement. Due to its ease of use, and due to the fact that both Internet Explorer 6 and Netscape 7 use this P3P feature in their cookie filtering tools, it has become very popular.

A compact policy is one line of code that will get you past the cookie filtering tools, especially when using third-party cookies. It requires only one request, unlike the full policy, which requires three. It is sent in the same HTTP header as the set-cookie response header field. As a developer, you will find it very easy to add a compact policy.

Here is a sample Java servlet, sent to us by our friend the Karate-site-manager and then anonymized:

```
package anon.karatesite.servlets;

import java.io.*;
import java.util.*;
import javax.servlet.*;
import javax.servlet.http.*;
import javax.naming.Context;
```

A Lesson on Cookie Filtering

A friend of ours called a few weeks ago, in the summer of 2002. He said something like "IE6 is blocking my cookies, and it says something about P3P. Can you help me?" It turned out that his karate site, which he, as a programmer, was managing in his spare time, used images at a domain other than the one the browser requested.

"You must add a compact policy to your cookie," we said. "This is a piece of code that might help."

He added the string to his Java servlet and wham! It worked! So we told him wisely: "Fine, now you must try to understand what these three-letter combinations mean, and make sure your site adheres to the privacy statement that you just made."

"Sure," he said. "But not today."

```
import javax.naming.InitialContext;
import anon.utils.*;
import anon.karatesite.beans.UserBean;
import anon.karatesite.businessobjects.*;

public class Test extends HttpServlet {

  /**
   * service method comment.
   */
  public void doGet(HttpServletRequest request, HttpServletResponse
response)
    throws ServletException, IOException{
    java.io.PrintWriter out = response.getWriter();
    HttpSession session = request.getSession(true);

    response.setContentType("text/html; charset=iso-8859-1");
    Cookie c = new Cookie("karatesite", "some text");
    c.setSecure(true);
    response.addCookie(c);

    response.addHeader("P3P","CP=\"CP="NOI DSP COR CUR ADM DEV PSAo PSDo
OUR BUS UNI PUR INT DEM STA PRE COM NAV OTC\"");

    String uri = request.getRequestURI();
    String service = uri.substring(uri.lastIndexOf("/")+1);
    out.println("Servlet: " + uri);
    out.println("Service: " + service);
    out.println("QS: "  + request.getQueryString());

  }}
```

As you can see, the response.addHeader element contains a string of code, which is in essence the compact policy:

```
P3P: CP="NOI DSP COR CUR ADM DEV PSAo PSDo OUR BUS UNI PUR INT DEM STA
PRE COM NAV OTC"
```

We will not describe what the rest of the example code means because this is not a crash course in Java programming. Instead, let's take a look at how the policy works in the two leading browsers.

Example of a Third-party Cookie That Uses a Compact Policy

When surfing to a specific site, an advertisement company set, or tried to set, a cookie through a banner. In the Netscape 7 cookie manager, we allowed the cookie to be set and then viewed all the information that was stored regarding this cookie. See Figure 10.2.

Netscape 7 provides you with the possibility to read the compact policy of the cookie after it has been set. We have not discovered this functionality in IE6, which appears to display it only when the prompt for cookies is selected.

In the bottom field of Figure 10.2, you can see the English interpretation of the compact policy.

We went to the same site using Internet Explorer 6, but this time using the prompt for cookies, and we got back the information shown in Figure 10.3.

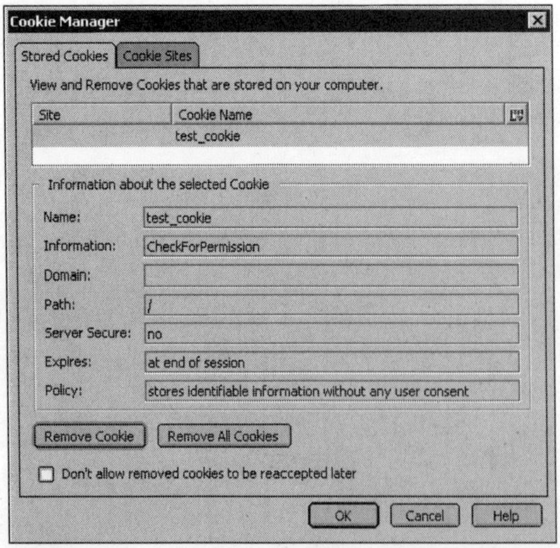

Figure 10.2. Netscape 7 Cookie Manager.

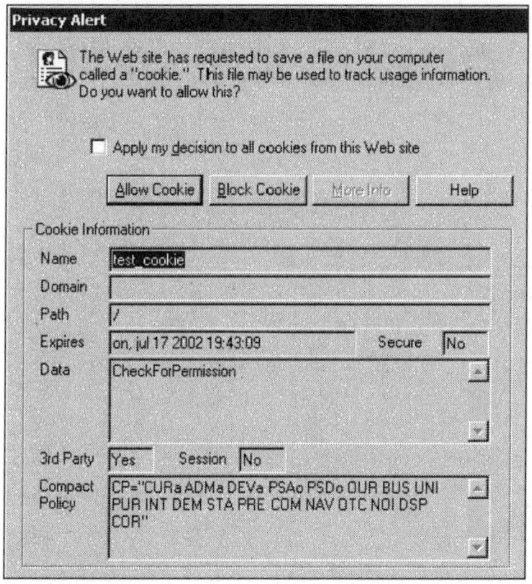

Figure 10.3. Internet Explorer 6 Privacy Alert.

As shown in the IE6 Privacy Alert screen in Figure 10.3, the compact policy is not interpreted at all, but we can see it the way the programmer wrote it. If we were to select Block Cookie here, we would see a blocked cookie sign at the bottom of the browser.

The information missing in both implementations is the value of the cookie; see Chapter 4. The value, though, is probably not so interesting—it is usually just an incomprehensible string anyway. If you want to see it, look at the example at the beginning of this chapter.

The Implications of the Three-Letter Combinations

A compact policy starts with:

```
CP=""
```

Between the quotation marks is a set of tokens. The order of the tokens is insignificant. You can mix them any way you choose. We describe them here in the same order as we did in Chapter 9.

Table 10.1 Access Tokens

TOKEN	CORRESPONDING TAG
NOI	<nonident/>
ALL	<all/>
CAO	<contact-and-other/>
IDC	<ident-contact/>
OTI	<other-ident/>
NON	<none/>

ACCESS

Will you grant users access to the information about them that you have collected?

You can use one or several of the three-letter combinations found in Table 10.1. Some combinations obviously do not make sense semantically in the same policy, such as combining ALL and NON.

Assume that you have a site where your advertisers, or advertising brokers, want to use their banners to set cookies. The cookies will facilitate ad rotation, recognize frequent users, and allow the advertisers to draw statistics from users' surf patterns. We will now create a sample policy that they can use:

```
CP="NOI"
```

No identified data is used.

DISPUTES

If you have a <DISPUTES-GROUP> in your full P3P policy, you can choose to add a DSP token to your policy, indicating that there is more information about how to settle disputes.

Assume that your advertisers have a full P3P policy with a disputes group. Our policy now looks like this:

```
CP="NOI DSP"
```

REMEDIES

The remedies in a compact policy can be <correct>, <money>, and/or <law>, indicating what you will do if you did something wrong. The three tokens are shown in Table 10.2:

Table 10.2 Remedies Tokens

TOKEN	CORRESPONDING TAG	EXPLANATION
COR	<correct/>	Errors or wrongful actions arising in connection with the privacy policy will be remedied by the service.
MON	<money/>	If the service provider violates its privacy policy, it will pay the individual an amount specified in the human-readable privacy policy or the amount of damages.
LAW	<law/>	Remedies for breaches of the policy statement will be determined based on the law referenced in the human-readable description.

You can use none, one, two, or all three of them. In our example, we use the <correct> token.

```
CP="NOI DSP COR"
```

NONIDENTIFIABLE

If we do not collect personal identifiable information, then we can add an NID (Non-IDentifiable) token to the statement. Because we already have an NOI, this would make sense. In the example that we are using, we are, confusingly enough, using an NOI but not an NID. The reason is that there is a lower threshold for an NOI, whose description says identified, than for an NID, which says identifiable. If a database contains information that could relate back to the user but does not do it directly, then obviously you cannot be expected to do data mining just to grant the user access to the identifiable data. Thus, for an NOI it is enough that the data is not directly related to a specific user, wheras for an NID, it needs to be almost impossible to trace the data back.

We would argue that there is no way you can place an NID in your policy if you are setting a persistent cookie and storing its value between the sessions, even if you do not log any data besides the cookie value. This, however, is just our opinion.

If we have an NID in our compact policy, then we would not have to state a purpose, recipient, and retention policy for the cookie. We do not have to add the NID at all, so we will leave the NID out of our example. Then the example policy is still the following code:

```
CP="NOI DSP COR"
```

PURPOSE

One of the biggest criticisms about cookies is that it has not been possible to tie a purpose to a cookie—thus, the user has no possibility of knowing for what it is used. This is solved with P3P. The possible tokens can be found in Table 10.3

You can also add an "a," "i," or "o" to the token, if you will be providing the end user with the possibility to opt in or opt out:

- *a* always indicates default, so you do not really need to add it; it indicates that there is no way not to have this information collected.
- *o* means that if the user bothers to go to the opt-out site as specified in the full policy, then the user can opt out of this collection.
- *i* means that the user can ask to have data collected (however, we do not see this being used in combination with cookies any time soon). This attribute cannot be used together with CUR, according to the specification.

Table 10.3 Purpose Tokens

TOKEN	CORRESPONDING TAG
CUR	<current/>
ADM	<admin/>
DEV	<develop/>
TAI	<tailoring/>
PSA	<pseudo-analysis/>
PSD	<pseudo-decision/>
IVA	<individual-analysis/>
IVD	<individual-decision/>
CON	<contact/>
HIS	<historical/>
TEL	<telemarketing/>
OTP	<other-purpose> *enter description within the tag* </other-purpose>

Because "a" is the default and "i" is unlikely to be used and cannot be used with CUR, we could say that the following PURPOSE tokens are valid:

CUR, ADM, DEV, TAI, PSA, PSD, IVA, IVD, CON, HIS, TEL, OTP, ADMo, DEVo, TAIo, PSAo, PSDo, IVAo, IVDo, CONo, HISo, TELo, and OTPo.

In our example, we use CUR for current, ADM for administration, and DEV for development purposes. They are mandatory. Your advertiser also uses pseudonymized data for analyses but offers the possibility to opt out of these. Thus, we add PSAo and PSDo to our compact policy.

```
CP="NOI DSP COR CUR ADM DEV PSAo PSDo"
```

RECIPIENT

The recipient or recipients of the information that can be redrawn from the placing of a cookie have five values. The possibility to opt out (or opt in) is also available for all recipients except OUR because that means that there are no other recipients.

Remember that the policy does apply not only to information that is stored in the cookie alone but also to information that can be collected because the cookie was set.

As you may recall from the Web bugs descriptions in Chapter 4, a third-party cookie provider can trace users across sites and store information about the users' habits. Look at the business model featured in Figure 10.4:

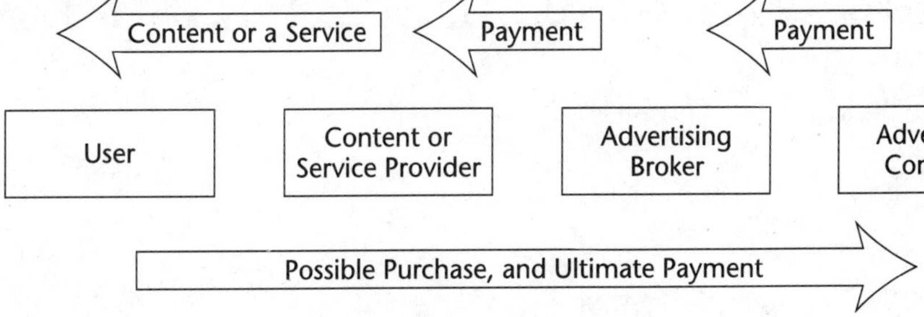

Figure 10.4 Internet business model.

The content or service provider gets paid by the advertising broker, and in return, he or she allows the banners on his or her site. The advertising broker provides space for banners at sites that have lots of hits, plus software for directed advertisement and ad rotation, which is very much based on the information that comes from the setting of the third-party cookies. Still, it is based on more than this information alone.

The advertising broker has a huge user database that contains a lot of information logs about end users—a tremendous benefit to the advertising company that wishes to use the broker. The company will be given nice presentations about where the ads will be placed, and it will be told that the ads are directed so that mainly users with an interest in the company's products will see them. Then what? Will the company want proof?

The advertising company can often recognize that a user visited its site by linking from an advertisement placed by the broker because the link or history will show this. Assuming that the user will actually buy something from the advertising company, and thus reveal his or her identity, can the advertising company ask the advertising broker questions about the user? Or will the advertising broker, when redirecting the user's request to the advertising company, add information about the user in the request?

If that is the case, it has to be stated in the selected tags, and OUR cannot be used.

Table 10.4 Recipient Tokens

TOKEN	CORRESPONDING TAG
OUR	<ours>
DEL	<delivery>
SAM	<same>
UNR	<other-recipient>
PUB	<unrelated>
OTR	<public>

The total list of reasonable useful tokens, omitting those with "i" and "a", would then be the following:

OUR, DEL, SAM, UNR, PUB, OTR, DELo, SAMo, UNRo, PUBo, OTRo

We assume that our advertiser does not share personal information, so our policy now says:

```
CP="NOI DSP COR CUR ADM DEV PSAo PSDo OUR"
```

RETENTION

The retention policy states the practices for retention, not the amount of time the data is stored.

From your advertiser's natural-language policy, you can find a link to a retention policy stating for each data element how long it is kept and how it is destroyed. Thus, we can add BUS from Table 10.5 in our compact policy example:

```
CP="NOI DSP COR CUR ADM DEV PSAo PSDo OUR BUS"
```

Categories

All the data collection that has anything to do with the cookie in question should be categorized and made part of the compact policy. The categories available are the same ones we defined in Chapter 7 and Chapter 9.

Table 10.5 Retention Tokens

TOKEN	CORRESPONDING TAG
NOR	<no-retention/>
STP	<stated-purpose/>
LEG	<legal-requirement/>
BUS	<business-practices/>
IND	<indefinitely/>

Table 10.6 Categories Tokens

TOKEN	CORRESPONDING TAG	EXPLANATION
PHY	<physical/>	**Physical contact information**: Information that allows an individual to be contacted or located in the physical world—such as a telephone number or an address.
ONL	<online/>	**Online contact information**: Information that allows an individual to be contacted or located on the Internet—such as an email address. Often, this information is independent of the specific computer used to access the network. (See the category "Computer information.")
UNI	<uniqueid/>	**Unique identifiers**: Nonfinancial identifiers, excluding government-issued identifiers, issued for purposes of consistently identifying or recognizing the individual. These include identifiers issued by a Web site or service.
PUR	<purchase/>	**Purchase information**: Information actively generated by the purchase of a product or service, including information about the method of payment.
FIN	<financial/>	**Financial information**: Information about an individual's finances including account status and activity information such as account balance, payment or overdraft history, and information about an individual's purchase or use of financial instruments including credit or debit card information. Information about a discrete purchase by an individual, as described in "Purchase information," alone does not come under the definition of "Financial information."
COM	<computer/>	**Computer information**: Information about the computer system that the individual is using to access the network—such as the IP number, domain name, browser type, or operating system.

Table 10.6 *(Continued)*

TOKEN	CORRESPONDING TAG	EXPLANATION
NAV	<navigation/>	**Navigation and clickstream data**: Data passively generated by browsing the Web site—such as which pages are visited and how long users stay on each page.
INT	<interactive/>	**Interactive data**: Data actively generated from or reflecting explicit interactions with a service provider through its site—such as queries to a search engine or logs of account activity.
DEM	<demographic/>	**Demographic and socioeconomic data**: Data about an individual's characteristics—such as gender, age, and income.
CNT	<content/>	**Content**: The words and expressions contained in the body of a communication—such as the text of email, bulletin board postings, or chat room communications.
STA	<state/>	**State management mechanisms**: Mechanisms for maintaining a stateful session with a user or automatically recognizing users who have visited a particular site or accessed particular content previously—such as HTTP cookies.
POL	<political/>	**Political information**: Membership in or affiliation with groups such as religious organizations, trade unions, professional associations, political parties, etc.
HEA	<health/>	**Health information**: Information about an individual's physical or mental health, sexual orientation, use or inquiry into health care services or products, and purchase of health care services or products.
PRE	<preference/>	**Preference data**: Data about an individual's likes and dislikes—such as favorite color or musical tastes.

(continues)

Table 10.6 Categories Tokens *(Continued)*

TOKEN	CORRESPONDING TAG	EXPLANATION
LOC	<location/>	**Location data**: Information that can be used to identify an individual's current physical location and track that person as his or her location changes—such as GPS position data.
GOV	<government/>	**Government-issued identifiers**: Identifiers issued by a government for purposes of consistently identifying the individual.
OTC	<other-category> string </other-category>	**Other**: Other types of data not captured by the preceding definitions. (A human-readable explanation should be provided in these instances, between the <other-category> and the </other-category> tags.)

Remember that the categories in Table 10.6 are *not* meant to specify the purpose of the data retention—only the kinds of data collected.

Here is our example policy:

```
CP="NOI DSP COR CUR ADM DEV PSAo PSDo OUR BUS UNI PUR INT DEM STA PRE
COM NAV OTC"
```

Add `P3P:` in front of the policy and you are done. It is now ready to be deployed.

```
P3P: CP="NOI DSP COR CUR ADM DEV PSAo PSDo OUR BUS UNI PUR INT DEM STA
PRE COM NAV OTC"
```

Legislation

If you write something in the compact policy that is not a P3P token, it will be disregarded by the user-agent. This is standard behavior for many languages—a way to ensure forward compatibility. That is, if there will be a future need for new tags, older tools should not stop functioning.

People use this feature to get away from the legal requirements that a P3P policy might impose as a contract. Add a token or a link to a statement saying, "I do this only to get past your user-agent, it is not true," and then no one can sue you if you break the policy.

Lawyers argue whether this is legal, and it remains to be seen what will happen when the first legal cases appear. We hope that we have shown that enhancing your Web site's privacy and then creating a statement that is valid is easier than lying. Without moralizing too much about this, it is safe to say that a good policy that is obeyed will earn you or your customers more respect from the public than cheating will.

Cookie Alternatives

HTTP is stateless—that is the problem. One request comes to the Web server, one response comes back, and all is forgotten. HTTP was not constructed to maintain sessions or to remember the user between sessions. Cookies were created to fulfill that need. Now, many programmers who base their programs on the use of cookies are frustrated because more and more users turn them off to protect their privacy.

If you do not want to use cookies, there are alternatives. The alternatives discussed in the following sections are in no way better at protecting the user's privacy; they are simply means to create applications for users who do not want cookies.

If you do decide to use cookies anyway, remember two things:

- Do not store any data in the cookie. Simply use it as an identifier—that is, send a dummy number and keep that number as a reference to the user. Whatever data you want to store in the cookie should be stored on the server instead. Keep it in a database if you have to. And if, for some reason, you really do need to store data in the cookie, encrypt it! Some Web sites store the user's name, identity, and even credit card number in cookies. All that stored data, especially in shared computers (think of all the users sharing computers at Internet cafés and libraries), is a threat to privacy.
- One cookie is enough. If you get a cookie with the request, you should not set another one.

The important question is what you are using the cookies for—maintaining a session using session cookies, or recognizing the user on his or her next visit using persistent cookies.

Session Cookies

There are roughly two types of sessions,:

- Ad-hoc sessions
- Login sessions

Ad hoc sessions

With ad hoc sessions, cookies are usually used to grant the user a better experience, and the session can then be built on the IP number because it is not likely that the number will be changed during the session. But if the IP number does change, it does not really matter that much. If you are not using links, but the HTTP POST method, you can add information about the user in hidden fields and thus maintain the session. Using the HTTP GET method, you can also add parameters, though this is usually a bit uglier because it will show in the links. This problem, however, is solved if you use frames.

Login sessions

With sessions that require login, cookies should not be used to ensure the user's identity unless the session is over a secure link—that is, unless SSL, TLS, or something similar (see Chapter 2) is used. With these sessions you can use the secure protocol to check the identity of the user for each request.

Web sites usually rely on a secure protocol only during authorization and then go back to nonsecure HTTP. This is a weak method, one that, for security reasons, should not be used unless the user is asked to identify himself or herself each time an action takes place that requires stronger identification. For example, a stockbroker might have a public part of his or her site where he or she uses session cookies to remember choices that the user makes during the session, such as words that were typed in. Within the part that requires login, information is available only to customers: information about the portfolio that the user has, plus an opportunity to sell and buy stocks and warrants. It is not terribly important that the information published about different stocks is not shown to nonclients. If a hacker bothered to do a man-in-the-middle attack by grabbing the cookie of the user, for example, and then using it with his or her own requests to pretend to be the user, no real harm is done. With login, the identification of the user relies on cookies or HTTP parameters, sent with the GET or POST requests.

When it comes to viewing the user's portfolio, it is more important that a proper identification scheme is used, and when it comes to placing an order, use of the proper scheme is extremely important. In both cases we are dealing not only with the user's privacy, but also with the non-repudiation factor. That is, the user must be held accountable for what he or she does, in case the user claims it was not he or she who did it.

Making the user sign each order is one way to achieve accountability. If you are using either a pin code generator or a client that the user has installed that is based on PKI or something similar, then you have achieved accountability. Otherwise, the method is probably not good enough. Most Web site owners realize that accountability is about taking a risk (that is, accepting a loss, if any) or about using a complicated method (and being able to make the user accept any loss). You have already made the choice, presumably.

When we are ensuring Greta's identity using session cookies or IP number-based sessions, or using HTTP GET or POST parameters to ensure that only Greta can view the stocks in her portfolio, it should be stated that none of the methods is secure in itself.

Thus, you do not really need cookies for maintaining sessions. They are too easy to forge to ensure the user's identification, and there are good alternatives if the identification of the user is not that important.

Persistent Cookies

Why are you using persistent cookies? Is it to keep track of the user's moves in order to tailor applications, to extract statistics, to rotate ads, or to provide the user with a better experience? Whatever the purpose, you have probably already decided that the benefits of using cookies justify their use. So, how do you reach the users who do not want to use persistent cookies?

One thing that you should remember is that the use of persistent cookies never gives you reliable identification of the user. You should never give away private information about a user, for example, simply because you get a cookie back. Imagine that you are running a stock broker site and that you greet the user by saying "Sorry, Greta, you lost five hundred today," and it is Greta's husband, colleague, neighbor, or some stranger in the coffee shop who is coming to the site. We advise that you do not assume anything about the user until proper identification has taken place.

Still, cookies are the best way to ensure that the user is the user. Using the IP number for user recognition is even more insecure because many big companies or Internet Service Providers (ISPs) rotate, or rather reuse, the numbers.

If the recognition of the user is important, and if you do not want the user to log in, you should set a persistent cookie only after having informed the user that this cookie is set because you want to recognize him or her the next time he or she visits and that the user should refuse the cookie if he or she is sharing the computer with someone—unless the Internet Service Provider (ISP) or company is using account-based cookies instead of computer-based cookies. We have never seen this implemented anywhere by a Web site, but it would be nice.

What would be even better would be to have a pop-up window in the user-agent saying that a site wishes to store a persistent cookie for these particular reasons and asking if that is OK with the user. In order to have such a tool, it is, of course, necessary to have a standardized language for tying a purpose, a retention policy, and everything else to the cookie.

Did you notice? We just invented P3P.

Cookie Policy Receipts—A Suggestion

The use of cookies within European countries will be allowed only *if the subscriber or user concerned is provided with clear and comprehensive information about the purpose of the cookies and is offered the right to refuse cookies*, according to European legal directives. It is not yet completely clear what effects this will have on the Web sites where the cookies originate. It is obvious that a policy needs to exist somewhere on the site.

Is a link to a natural-language policy placed at the bottom of what is presumably the entrance page enough? Well, we must assume that what is presumably the entrance page does not place any cookies itself. Otherwise, the cookie will be set before the user has a chance to find the policy. Obviously, a response carrying a policy should *never* set a cookie.

Still, how is the right to refuse cookies exercised? As Web site programmers, you could give the user the right to refuse cookies, but you will not be able to recognize the user because the user does not use cookies. Apparently, you could use IP number recognition, but still, the next time, it will be the same problem again.

How can the user opt out of the use of cookies? Through an opt-out page that is linked to from a link to the policy file? For each session? The discussion may sound a bit ridiculous. It is 10 times easier for the user to use a cookie filtering tool. Still, the law will place obligations on the owner of a European Web site.

P3P in itself is not enough. We can state that once and for all. The reason is that P3P user-agents are still very rare. If you as a Web site programmer knew that the P3P policy was read and understood by the user or by an agent that is aware of the user preferences, then you could happily place whatever cookies you want. You have provided a user-agent with clear and comprehensive information, and the user-agent gave the user the chance to opt out.

A cookie policy receipt mechanism is what is needed, in our opinion. The mechanism cannot be implemented in a compact policy because the policy is sent with the same request as the one setting the policy. It can be sent, though, with a regular P3P agreement; see Figure 10.1 in the beginning of the chapter.

Going back to the description at the beginning of the chapter, imagine the following:

A separate request is sent for both the reference file and the policy file, and the files come back with the responses. The policy includes cookie statements, which are read and matched with the user's preferences. Possibly, the user is asked in person whether he or she wants to retrieve the page, depending on the user's personal settings. With the final request for the actual resource—that is, the desired page—a cookie-policy-receipt is sent with the HTTP header, possibly resembling the following::

```
P3P: cookie-receipt-user-ok
```

Table 10.7 is an example of how this flag can be varied:

Table 10.7 Cookie-Receipts

RECEIPT	MEANING	ACTION BY USER-AGENT BEFORE SENDING	ACTION BY SERVER BEFORE SENDING SET-COOKIE
P3P: cookie-receipt-user-ok	The user was presented with the policy, and the user said it was OK to set one.	If there are any cookies stored on the server, they are sent with the receipt.	A set-cookie response header can be sent together with the content, and no additional information should need to be presented to the user.
P3P: cookie-receipt-prefs-ok	The policy was matched with the user's preferences, and it was OK.	If there are any cookies stored on the server, they are sent with the receipt.	A set-cookie response header can be sent together with the content, and no additional information should need to be presented to the user. However, because the user has not read the policy in person, info could be written in clear text.
P3P: cookie-receipt-user-nok	The user was asked and said no.	Cookies stored on the server are removed, and if the server sends a set-cookie response (which should be illegal, or at least immoral), it is ignored.	No set-cookie response header should be sent. A note can be pre sented to the user saying, "Because you refused cookies, the service will not function at all/fully..."
P3P: cookie-receipt-prefs-nok	The user's preferences were inconsistent with the policy of the service provider.	Cookies stored on the server are removed, and if the server sends a set-cookie response (which should be illegal, or at least immoral), it is ignored.	No set-cookie response header should be sent. A note can be pre sented to the user saying, "Because your preferences are set to refuse cookies, the service will not function at all/fully..."

This method is not yet used by any user-agent, but it would be a very good way to use P3P to ensure that European legislation is followed, we think.

Summary

In this chapter, we have explained how compact and full policies are created in P3P. In the next chapter, we discuss P3P user-agents.

Additional Reading

http://www.w3.org/P3P	The P3P site
http://www.w3.org/TR/P3P	The P3P specification
http://www.ietf.org/rfc/rfc1766.txt	Tags for the identification of languages

CHAPTER 11

User-Agents and Other P3P Tools

There are already a number of P3P tools out there. In this chapter, we describe the most commonly used ones. New tools are likely to appear soon.

Policies

Throughout this book we have focused on learning how to make a Web site P3P compliant. As a summary of what has been covered, there are a number of files at a P3P-enabled site, as shown in Figure 11.1.

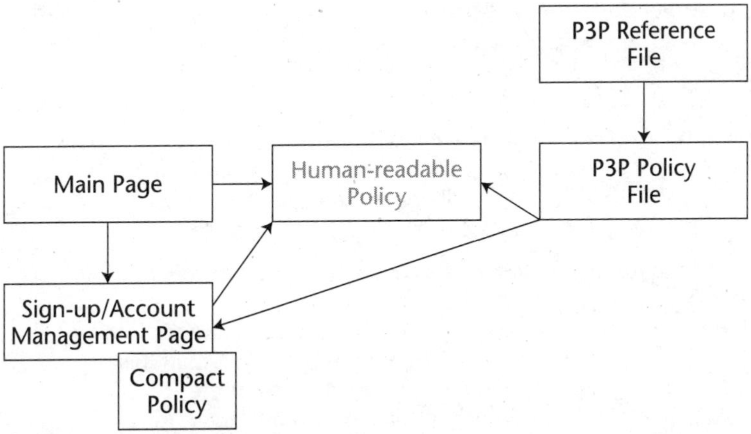

Figure 11.1. Relevant files at the content provider.

Let's take a look at an example of what a P3P-enabled site could look like. All the filenames and paths are suggestions, except the reference file. In this example, shown in Table 11.1, the site is in English.

Table 11.1 Paths of the Relevant Files

FILE AND PATH	COMMENT	LANGUAGE
www.werespectyou.com	This is the **main page**, and from here you can access any other page. No cookie will be set from this page at the first visit because the privacy policy file has not been accessed yet. At the bottom of this page, there is a link called Privacy Policy that will lead to the human-readable privacy policy file.	English
www.werespectyou.com/ myaccount/	The site has user accounts, and you can sign up and manage your personal data at this site through a **sign-up/account management page**. Because this page gives you the possibilities to opt in and opt out of some services, it is referred to from the P3P specification (see Chapter 9). It uses a cookie to recognize the user. The practices of this page are described both in the cookie compact policy and in the P3P policy file that is relevant to this part of the site. At the bottom of this page there is a link to the human-readable privacy policy file.	English
privacy.werespectyou.com	The privacy practices of the entire site are described in one **human-readable privacy policy** file (see Chapter 8).	English
www.werespectyou.com/ w3c/p3p.xml	The **P3P reference file** is always located at /w3c/p3p.xml, called the well-known location. It indicates where to find the P3P policy file.	XML
www.werespectyou.com/ w3c/policy.xml	Many sites reuse the w3c directory that they had to create in order to have a place for their P3P reference file to store the **P3P policy**. Within this policy, there is a link both to the opt-in/opt-out page and to the human-readable privacy policy.	XML

The content provider can use three kinds of tools to create its policies:

- P3P Policy Generator
- XML Validator
- P3P Validator

The first kind of tool that a Web site owner could have is a P3P Policy Generator. You may use it to write the XML for your P3P reference and policy files or to write your compact policies for you. Such a policy generator could create both the P3P policy file and the human-readable policy file.

Personally, we still write HTML by hand because we do not like the idea of letting anything generate tags for us. We do acknowledge that most people feel differently, though.

XML checkers are another kind of tool for creating P3P policies. They take your reference and policy files and check their validity. You can either use a traditional XML Validator and feed it with the P3P DTD (see Appendix A) or take a P3P Validator that checks only P3P files.

Client Side

Once all relevant files are in place at the service provider, there must be a client tool at the client side that can deal with those files. We first discuss what kinds of user-agents there are, or will be, and then look at a few of those that exist.

Viewers

The simplest kind of client-side tools are viewers. A viewer can present the following:

- The P3P policy file for the relevant page through the reference file (see Chapter 9)
- The compact policy file (see Chapter 10)
- The human-readable policy file via the P3P policy file (see Chapter 9)
- The opt-in/opt-out file via the P3P policy file

A viewer will not take any action, but simply on demand show the user what the policy is for the specific site.

User-Agents

A P3P user-agent is a more complete tool. It will not only present the file, but also use the fact that the policy is machine-readable to take some kind of action. We have already discussed cookie filtering tools in Chapter 10 and how you can use a P3P policy, compact or full, to block, prompt, or set a cookie.

The same kind of block, prompt, or get action can be taken for a whole page. Normally, though, a user will not want a page to be completely blocked, but only to be warned if there are inconsistencies between her privacy preferences and the policy that refers to the page in question.

To have a user-agent, user preferences must be stored somewhere. These must be created, preferably by the user—otherwise they would not be user preferences. There is a potential problem here—users will not want to create too many preferences. Thus, the user-agent should be like an expert system and learn from the user's choices.

You can place the following requirements on a P3P user-agent:

- It should contain a complete viewer, as described previously.
- It should contain an administration interface so that the user can add, delete, or update her privacy preferences.
- It should contain mechanisms to learn when the user makes decisions.
- It should be able to take actions when a page does not adhere to a user's preferences.

The question is, which actions should it take? As with cookie filtering tools, you can obviously block, prompt, or get a page. We can foresee other kinds of actions as well. A really good user-agent placed in a network could be combined with an anonymizer, so that a site with a bad policy or lacking a policy will get an anonymized request—that is, a request that contains a forged IP number—while the user gets a message warning him or her that "this is a bad place to be—do not give anything away!"

A good P3P user-agent should know whether it is important to read the P3P policy at all. If, for example, the user uses a banking service or a stockbroker, it may not be relevant to know what kinds of practices they have because they already have all your data anyway. You have already made a decision that this site is always reliable. This is possible to specify using the Request-group attribute in APPEL.

A user-agent should handle stored cookies, so that if a policy is not compliant with the user's settings because the policy or the user preferences changed, existing cookies should be removed. It should contain history lists and log files, and most importantly, the user-agent must be a tool that is completely trusted by the user, reliable, and easy to use.

Intermediary Servers

An intermediary server is a place that a request passes through before being sent to the client, like a party sitting in the middle talking to the person on the left and passing the word on to the person on the right. There are several reasons for using one, including networking reasons or policy reasons. Intermediary servers that read an HTTP request and pass it on are called HTTP proxies—we discussed these in Chapter 3.

An HTTP proxy can be placed at the ISP, at a telecom operator, or within a company. P3P user-agents can act as such a proxy. There are many benefits with network user-agents:

- If the connection from the proxy to the user is slow for some reason (for instance, if the user is using a phone line or a mobile device), it is faster to let the proxy handle the greater part of the traffic.
- It is often cheaper to install one tool and update it when new versions come up than to install and maintain a tool at each client.
- It is less memory- and processor-consuming to use one tool.
- If you use different clients, the account you have with the central tool can be used regardless of where you are.

The drawback is that this tool will know so much about you. If your data is stolen, you will end up with less privacy than you had in the first place. You should remember that if you are using a secure connection, it is usually tunneled through a proxy—an HTTP proxy will not see the traffic, but only pass it on. If you want the P3P user-agent proxy to make wise decisions, you will have to let the proxy see the data. In other words, you will establish a secure link to the proxy, and you will link the proxy to the site. This is an obvious security breach.

We predict that companies will invest in P3P user-agent proxies at some point, and we hope that they will do this wisely.

P3P for Data Conveyance

We have a suggestion for future user-agent developers: P3P can be used for data conveyance. This idea is part of the research that is presented in Appendix B, "Taking Charge of Profile Information Conveyance." The paper was written with mobile devices as target user-agents, but it could just as well apply to regular clients.

The idea is to use the powerful language of P3P to say "Give me your data and I will . . ." rather than "If you would give me your data, I will . . .".

After the policy file is sent to the client, the client will not only decide whether or not to block, prompt, GET, or anonymize, but also send the data that the policy describes in the HTTP header.

This, in turn, suggests that the user has a profile stored in the agent, containing personal information about himself or herself—such as name and address; user-agent information, like browser-name or Bluetooth version; other preferences like "I don't want images, just give me the text"; personal interests, like sport but not music; or even a credit card number. All this information can be baked into the HTTP header and transmitted with the request.

The format for conveying user data in our example is Composite Capabilities and Preference Profile (CC/PP), about which you can read more at the W3C site (www.w3.org).

Look at the following scenario:

- Greta has her name and address stored in a profile.
- She goes to werespectyou.com to order a violin.
- Her user-agent fetches the site's privacy policy.
- It is OK to surf around—no alert.
- She goes to the specific site where it asks for her name, address, and credit card number.

- She gets a warning from her user-agent, stating exactly what the site wants, for what purpose, and its retention policy and all the other stuff that a policy can tell you (as covered in Chapter 9).
- Greta knows why it is asking—she just ordered—and now she has learned about the site's policy, and she then clicks OK.
- Within the request header comes all the information needed:

```
<?xml version="1.0"?>
<RDF xmlns="http://www.w3.org/1999/02/22-rdf-syntax-ns#"
xmlns:rdf="http://www.w3.org/1999/02/22-rdf-syntax-ns#"
xmlns:prf="http://www.mysite.org/Buddies/ccppschema-20020727#">
        <rdf:Description ID="Profile">
                <prf:component>
                        <rdf:Description ID="UserData">
                                <prf:Gender>Female</prf:Gender>
                                <prf:Age>27</prf:Age>
                                <prf:Languages>
                                        <rdf:Bag>

<rdf:li>Swedish</rdf:li>

<rdf:li>English</rdf:li>
                                                <rdf:li>German</rdf:li>

<rdf:li>Russian</rdf:li>

<rdf:li>Spanish</rdf:li>
                                        </rdf:Bag>
                                </prf:Languages>
                                <prf:Name>Greta</prf:Name>
                                <prf:Location>Stockholm</prf:Location>
                                <prf:JobTitle>Warrants-
Consultant</prf:JobTitle>
                        </rdf:Description>
                </prf:component>
        </rdf:Description>
</RDF>
```

- The servlet or CGI script that receives her request notices that there is a data-conveyance-compliant user-agent at the other end and accepts the data without asking Greta to fill in a form. Instead it prefills the form and sends it back for acceptance.

Data conveyance means convenience for the user. Such convenience is always a benefit, but it is especially important in mobile environments.

Existing P3P Tools

The goal of this chapter has been to show what kinds of user-agents there might be available for you to consider. We have focused on the generic parts. Now we look a little more closely at what is available as of the writing of this book.

Validators

At the P3P Toolbox site, http://p3ptoolbox.org/, you can find lists of available P3P tools, as well as other useful information. There you can find tools both to create and to validate policies. You can also sign up for mailing lists and read other people's questions and comments.

We strongly recommend that you check your policy file or compact policy through several validators. If there is a mistake somewhere, the correct user-agent behavior is to disregard it completely, as opposed to standard browsing behavior, which is error correction. It is not clear whether this requirement from the P3P specification, which was widely discussed, will be adhered to by all the user-agents, which is why you should try several user-agents or validators before deciding that your policy is OK.

As an exercise, try to run the compact policy that we created in Chapter 10 through the validator that you will find at that site. You can see its English interpretation as well as its compliance with Internet Explorer 6.

User-Agents and Viewers

We have already discussed the P3P implementations of the most frequently used Web browsers, namely Internet Explorer 6 and Netscape 7 in Chapter 10. They contain cookie filtering tools, where one of the filtering conditions is the existence of a P3P policy and the content of this policy. They also contain viewers, where you can read both the human-readable policy and the P3P policy. For more information, please see Microsoft's and Netscape's Web sites.

There are also several P3P user-agents available that have been developed in research projects. One such agent is the AT&T Privacy Bird, which is described at the W3C site.

Another interesting user-agent is the Joint Research Center (JRC) P3P Demonstrator Tool. It is a proxy, developed by a research group whose members are working in the APPEL group to be a complete user preferences tool. You can really do everything with this tool—that is, you can set it up exactly as you want. It does require some knowledge from the users, which is OK, because it is a research tool. We imagine that this will be helpful for nonprogrammers who want to get a good understanding of everything there is to know about a privacy preference.

The JRC User-Agent

The Joint Research Center of the European Commission has provided a suite of tools for understanding and evaluating P3P.

1. User Agent Proxy Service

   This is a proxy service, meaning that you do not have to download any software or use any particular browser. You just configure your browser to make requests to the Internet through the JRC proxy service (available from p3p.jrc.it). Your browsing experience is then much the same as usual except that you will receive a small expandable P3P menu with every page, which allows you to do the following:

   a. View information on the P3P evaluation that has been made for every page.

   b. Switch identities, which are sets of preferences that you can either define yourself using APPEL files or choose from a predefined set, including one that aims to protect you to the minimum level of European law.

   c. Create new identities.

   d. View help on the proxy.

   Furthermore, according to the APPEL rules that you have specified, pages or resources may be blocked (for instance, harmful cookies or images), or you may receive warning pop-ups.

2. A model P3P site. In conjunction with the user agent, this can be used to try out various key scenarios for P3P.

   The proxy requires you to authenticate yourself when you start a session or view information about how the service has handled your pages, and your privacy preferences are private to you and should not be viewed by anyone else.

3. Local "Proxy" Agent

   This is the same as the proxy service, but it works on your own machine and therefore does not require a login and may perform better. Instead of configuring your browser to work through the JRC machine, you configure it to use the local Java application as a proxy so that all requests are filtered through this application instead of the remote proxy. Effectively it is the same as a browser plug-in, but it cannot alter the look of your browser and it works across all browsers.

4. P3P Toolkit

   This includes the folloing:

   - A complete set of documentation on P3P
   - A copy of the JRC Preference GUI
   - Sample preference files
   - An application for testing policies against rule-sets according to APPEL/P3P, independently of a user agent

5. APPEL Evaluator Module

   This is the Java code for making decisions on policies according to rule-sets. It is used in the proxy, but this is the code for the separate module that can be plugged into any user agent.

6. APPEL Preference GUI

   This is a complete graphical user interface for creating and editing APPEL rules. It is the only interface available that supports the full range of options available in APPEL. It is divided into a "pick a rule" section, designed for basic users, and a full interface, designed for advanced users such as data commissioners. It is envisaged that this interface could be used to create and distribute standard preferences sets for people who do not have the time to study the complex questions regarding which preferences to set.

Summary

This chapter has discussed the tools available in 2002. In the next chapter, we talk about P3P and the mobile Internet.

Additional Reading

http://www.w3.org/P3P	The P3P site
http://p3ptoolbox.org/tools/resources1.shtml	A collection of P3P user-agents and other tools
http://www.w3.org/TR/CCPP-trust/	CC/PP Implementer's Guide: Privacy and Protocols
http://www.w3.org/TR/CCPP-struct-vocab/	Composite Capability/Preference Profiles (CC/PP): Structure and Vocabularies
http://www.openmobilealliance.org/	Open Mobile Alliance
http://www.w3.org/P3P/validator.html	The W3C P3P Validator
www.jrc.it	Joint Research Center in Italy

CHAPTER 12

P3P and the Mobile Internet

Privacy in mobile environments has the same base aspects as privacy in the legacy Internet. Within this chapter, we discuss the specific features of the mobile Internet, why these put the privacy of the end users at risk, why this risk must be considered if the mobile Internet is to take off, and how to begin solving the privacy problems.

Mobile Internet—The Vision

The Mobile Internet is about accessing content from a mobile device, such as a cellular phone or a PDA over the air. The services provided could be anything from:

- Online information such as news, stocks, and weather
- Pushed content (like SMS, but from a Push server)
- Downloads (games, content, music)
- HTTP-based clients (downloaded or included)
- Chat services
- Location-based services like finding where the nearest restaurant or gas station is or reporting to a server that needs to know your whereabouts

- Internet-based services, such as banking, games, and ordering goods
  - Intranet-based services, such as Calendar, Mail, Contacts, and access printers and faxes
  - Bluetooth services such as direct payment (pay as you pass the cashier by typing in your pin code, instead of using a credit card) and synchronizing content with your PC

Any combination of the above is of course possible—for example, your bank could provide you with a downloadable HTTP client that you can use for regular banking services such as viewing your account, and buying and selling stocks, as well as transfering money to your daughter, who just sent you a picture of the jeans she wants to buy. This client will also enable you to use your device for Bluetooth payment services, because it can communicate directly with the bank itself.

We have worked with mobile Internet services since 1998—first with WAP, then with MeT—which is WAP services over Bluetooth—then with different angles of privacy and WAP, and all the time we have felt that the takeoff of mobile Internet is just around the corner. What is taking it so long? It is a combination of things—the services are not there, or at least they are good enough, it takes time for people to learn to use them, it is expensive, and it is slow among other things.

All that will get better, and mobile Internet will become popular. When it does, we believe that the privacy problems should have already been addressed.

Mobile Internet Architecture

Mobile Internet started with the Wireless Application Protocol (WAP) and the WAP Forum in 1997, as a joint initiative between Ericsson, Nokia, Motorola, and Unwired Planet (known today as OpenWave). Today, WAP Forum is part of Open Mobile Alliance (OMA), and the standard is converging with the traditional Internet protocols.

Regardless of the protocols used—WAP, iMode, or others—there are some generic features in a mobile Internet architecture:

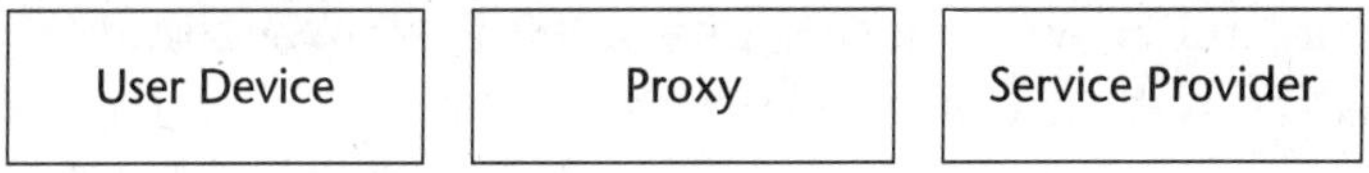

Figure 12.1 Relevant files at the content provider.

- A user device, which is different from the traditional PC or workstation
- A wireless connection to a telecom operator, which may hold a proxy or gateway
- A service provider that is mobile Internet compliant, see Figure 12-1.

The User Device

A number of features are common with most mobile Internet user devices:

- The device is personal in terms of being tied to one specific user much more than a PC is tied to the user.
- It is normally small, which implies that it has limited capabilities—a restricted keyboard, a small screen, and limited storage capacity.
- The device sends and receives data over the air, which means that communication to and from the device is slow. The link itself is insecure—sometimes it can be broken. Generally, communication is expensive.
- It contains some specific features, such as an alarm bell, a timer, a phone book, and ring tones.
- The user can also add a camera, an MP3 player, and other electronic gadgets to it.
- The very specific features, in terms of screen size, memory storage, and type of keyboard, make it unique, and they make it important to adjust the presentation of the content to suit the application. This user-agent profile is part of the device, and it is normally presented to the application.

The ease of portability with these types of devices means that the device is almost always with the user, no matter where the user goes; hence it has the same location as the user. The device might know this location, and the location is always, to some extent, known to the telecom operator.

The Proxy/Gateway

There was a WAP gateway, mainly for conversion between WAP and HTTP, in the original WAP specifications. Now it is optional, but there is still most likely a proxy somewhere on the telecom operator's premises. This proxy can handle things for the user, such as storing user profiles, adding the location to requests, adding the device profile to the request, or performing a P3P agreement. It can also be used for identity management and for single sign-on—that is, as the point of authentication for services—so that the user will not have to logon more than once.

We envision the telecom operator's network to be the place where the user will store all his or her privacy preferences. It is so convenient. He or she will not need to authenticate the operator because information about who the user is can be fetched from the lower layers. The user can then determine whether he or she wants to be anonymous with a service provider or use a pseudonym or full identification.

The telecom operator will be able to charge the user for actions taken on the Internet, possibly without knowing where the user went or what he or she did, and sometimes the party from whom the user purchases things does not need to know who the user is.

It is to some extent natural that the telecom operator will perform a P3P agreement for the user because that lowers the number of over-the-air transmissions. The device might just as well do this itself. In the latter case, the user will be in control. It is also possible that users will choose a combination where parts of the P3P user-agent will be in the device and the rest will be at the telecom operator's premises.

Sometimes the proxy/gateway will not be in the telecom operator's environment at all. Large companies may choose to have their own proxy behind their firewall performing some or all of the preceding tasks, turning the operator into a bit-pipe provider. If there is a Bluetooth connection, there will probably not be an intermediary party at all.

The Service Provider

The service provider will have to create pages written in Wireless Markup Language (WML), or rather a WML deck, XHTML, compact HTML (cHTML), or some other kind of language that is compliant with a mobile device. Those pages should be able to handle the differences in user device capabilities mentioned previously. Typically, your site will use the same set of policies if your site supports mobile Internet.

P3P-Enabling a WAP Site

In order to create a P3P-enabled mobile Internet platform, you must have the same software that you would need to set up a regular Web site—that is, a Web server. You also need a tagged language to create your application. In Japan, you might want to use cHTML for your iMode application; in the rest of the world, it would be XHTML or WML 2.0.

A WAP User-Agent Profile

The WAP user-agent profiles are described in specifications created by the WAP Forum, currently Open Mobile Alliance (OMA) (see http://www.oma.org/), and they are based on the CC/PP profile format, defined by the W3C, which in turn is based on the Resource Description Framework (RDF) specification. RDF is not XML, but a tagged language that is circular—that is, it will not be parsed into a tree, but into a graph. More information can be found at the W3C Web site.

The following is an example of a WAP user-agent profile, which will either be part of the request for resource or be pointed to by a URL in the HTTP or WSP header. It shows the device capabilities of an Ericsson R520 cellular phone, and its official URL is http://mobileinternet.ericsson.se/UAProf/R520.xml.

```
@

<?xml version="1.0"?>
<RDF xmlns="http://www.w3.org/1999/02/22-rdf-syntax-ns#"
xmlns:rdf="http://www.w3.org/1999/02/22-rdf-syntax-ns#"
xmlns:prf="http://www.wapforum.org/UAPROF/ccppschema-20000405#">
     <rdf:Description ID="Profile">
           <prf:component>
```

```
            <rdf:Description ID="HardwarePlatform">
                  <prf:ScreenSize>101x67</prf:ScreenSize>
                  <prf:Model>R520m</prf:Model>
                  <prf:InputCharSet>
                        <rdf:Bag>
                              <rdf:li>ISO-8859-1</rdf:li>
                              <rdf:li>US-ASCII</rdf:li>
                              <rdf:li>UTF-8</rdf:li>
                              <rdf:li>ISO-10646-UCS-
2</rdf:li>
                        </rdf:Bag>
                  </prf:InputCharSet>
                  <prf:ScreenSizeChar>15x6</prf:ScreenSizeChar>
                  <prf:BitsPerPixel>2</prf:BitsPerPixel>
                  <prf:ColorCapable>No</prf:ColorCapable>
                  <prf:TextInputCapable>Yes</prf:TextInputCa-
pable>
                  <prf:ImageCapable>Yes</prf:ImageCapable>
                  <prf:Keyboard>PhoneKeypad</prf:Keyboard>
                  <prf:NumberOfSoftKeys>0</prf:NumberOfSoftKeys>
                  <prf:Vendor>Ericsson Mobile Communications
AB</prf:Vendor>
                  <prf:OutputCharSet>
                        <rdf:Bag>
                              <rdf:li>ISO-8859-1</rdf:li>
                              <rdf:li>US-ASCII</rdf:li>
                              <rdf:li>UTF-8</rdf:li>
                              <rdf:li>ISO-10646-UCS-
2</rdf:li>
                        </rdf:Bag>
                  </prf:OutputCharSet>
                  <prf:SoundOutputCapable>Yes</prf:SoundOut-
putCapable>
                  <prf:StandardFontProportional>Yes</prf:Stan-
dardFontProportional>
                  <prf:PixelsAspectRatio>1x1,24</prf:Pixel-
sAspectRatio>
            </rdf:Description>
      </prf:component>
      <prf:component>
            <rdf:Description ID="SoftwarePlatform">

<prf:AcceptDownloadableSoftware>No</prf:AcceptDownloadableSoftware>
            </rdf:Description>
      </prf:component>
      <prf:component>
            <rdf:Description ID="NetworkCharacteristics">
                  <prf:SecuritySupport>WTLS class 1/2/3/sign-
Text</prf:SecuritySupport>
```

```
                              <prf:SupportedBearers>
                                     <rdf:Bag>
                                            <rdf:li>TwoWaySMS</rdf:li>
                                            <rdf:li>CSD</rdf:li>
                                            <rdf:li>GPRS</rdf:li>
                                     </rdf:Bag>
                              </prf:SupportedBearers>
                       </rdf:Description>
                </prf:component>
                <prf:component>
                       <rdf:Description ID="BrowserUA">
                              <prf:BrowserName>Ericsson</prf:BrowserName>
                              <prf:CcppAccept>
                                     <rdf:Bag>

<rdf:li>application/vnd.wap.wmlc</rdf:li>

<rdf:li>application/vnd.wap.wbxml</rdf:li>

<rdf:li>application/vnd.wap.wmlscriptc</rdf:li>

<rdf:li>application/vnd.wap.multipart.mixed</rdf:li>
                                            <rdf:li>text/x-vCard</rdf:li>
                                            <rdf:li>text/x-
vCalendar</rdf:li>
                                            <rdf:li>text/x-vMel</rdf:li>
                                            <rdf:li>text/x-
eMelody</rdf:li>

<rdf:li>image/vnd.wap.wbmp</rdf:li>
                                            <rdf:li>image/gif</rdf:li>

<rdf:li>application/vnd.wap.wtls-ca-certificate</rdf:li>

<rdf:li>application/vnd.wap.sic</rdf:li>

<rdf:li>application/vnd.wap.slc</rdf:li>

<rdf:li>application/vnd.wap.coc</rdf:li>

<rdf:li>application/vnd.wap.sia</rdf:li>
                                     </rdf:Bag>
                              </prf:CcppAccept>
                              <prf:CcppAccept-Charset>
                                     <rdf:Bag>
                                            <rdf:li>US-ASCII</rdf:li>
                                            <rdf:li>ISO-8859-1</rdf:li>
                                            <rdf:li>UTF-8</rdf:li>
                                            <rdf:li>ISO-10646-UCS-
2</rdf:li>
```

```
                    </rdf:Bag>
                </prf:CcppAccept-Charset>
                <prf:CcppAccept-Encoding>
                    <rdf:Bag>
                        <rdf:li>base64</rdf:li>
                    </rdf:Bag>
                </prf:CcppAccept-Encoding>
                <prf:FramesCapable>No</prf:FramesCapable>
                <prf:TablesCapable>Yes</prf:TablesCapable>
            </rdf:Description>
        </prf:component>
        <prf:component>
            <rdf:Description ID="WapCharacteristics">
                <prf:WapDeviceClass>C</prf:WapDeviceClass>
                <prf:WapPushMsgSize>3000</prf:WapPushMsgSize>
                <prf:WapVersion>1.2.1/June 2000</prf:WapVer-
sion>
                <prf:WmlVersion>
                    <rdf:Bag>
                        <rdf:li>1.2.1/June
2000</rdf:li>
                        <rdf:li>1.1</rdf:li>
                    </rdf:Bag>
                </prf:WmlVersion>
                <prf:WmlDeckSize>3000</prf:WmlDeckSize>
                <prf:WmlScriptVersion>
                    <rdf:Bag>
                        <rdf:li>1.2.1/June
2000</rdf:li>
                        <rdf:li>1.1</rdf:li>
                    </rdf:Bag>
                </prf:WmlScriptVersion>
                <prf:WmlScriptLibraries>
                    <rdf:Bag>
                        <rdf:li>Lang</rdf:li>
                        <rdf:li>Float</rdf:li>
                        <rdf:li>String</rdf:li>
                        <rdf:li>URL</rdf:li>
                        <rdf:li>WMLBrowser</rdf:li>
                        <rdf:li>Dialogs</rdf:li>
                    </rdf:Bag>
                </prf:WmlScriptLibraries>
                <prf:WtaiLibraries>
                    <rdf:Bag>
                        <rdf:li>WTA.Public.make-
Call</rdf:li>
                        <rdf:li>WTA.Public.send-
DTMF</rdf:li>
```

```
<rdf:li>WTA.Public.addPBEntry</rdf:li>
                                    </rdf:Bag>
                              </prf:WtaiLibraries>
                        </rdf:Description>
                  </prf:component>
      </rdf:Description>
</RDF>
```

When you create the P3P policy file as in Chapter 10, you may want to describe what to do with the preceding data, in which case you will not want to use just the data elements from the P3P specification.

Creating a P3P Policy for WAP Applications

We assume that you are dealing with more, or different, data in your WAP applications than at your regular Web site. This means that you will have to create separate policies for your mobile applications. You may not need to create a separate human-readable policy because it is easy to create a subsection describing what is different if you are using mobile applications.

Creating a Reference File

You can put your WAP applications in three places:

- At a different domain
- At the same domain, but a different path
- At the same path, depending on the presentation of the browser type

This all affects the creation of the reference file, of course. If you store all your WAP pages at a different domain, like wap.werespectyou.com, then you will need a new reference file, located at wap.werespectyou.com/w3c/p3p.xml.

If you are using the same domain but a different path, you will simply include this path in the existing policy file—let's reuse the reference file from Chapters 9 and 10:

```
<META xmlns="http://www.w3.org/2002/01/P3Pv1">
 <POLICY-REFERENCES>
  <EXPIRY max-age="86400"/>
```

```
    <POLICY-REF about="/P3P/default_policy.xml">
      <INCLUDE>/*</INCLUDE>
      <EXCLUDE>/register/index.html</EXCLUDE>
      <EXCLUDE>/purchase/index.html</EXCLUDE>
      <EXCLUDE>/wap/*</EXCLUDE>
    </POLICY-REF>

    <POLICY-REF about="/P3P/register_policy.xml">
      <INCLUDE>/register/index.html</INCLUDE>
      <COOKIE-INCLUDE/>
    </POLICY-REF>

    <POLICY-REF about="/P3P/purchase_policy.xml">
      <INCLUDE>/purchase/index.html</INCLUDE>
    </POLICY-REF>

    <POLICY-REF about="/P3P/cookie_policy.xml">
      <COOKIE-INCLUDE>/info/*</COOKIE-INCLUDE>
    </POLICY-REF>

    <POLICY-REF about="/P3P/mobileinternet_policy.xml">
      <INCLUDE>/wap/*</INCLUDE>
      <COOKIE-INCLUDE/>
    </POLICY-REF>

  </POLICY-REFERENCES>
</META>
```

As you can see, we assume that the WAP part of the site is setting cookies.

Some Web sites use the same URLs and applications regardless of the device requesting them. Instead they use the information that can be redrawn from the MIME type or the browser type to customize the presentation of the application.

In this case it is trickier creating a policy.

You can either decide to create one worst-case policy for all the applications, where you state what you will do the most, or else generate or redirect the reference file, too. A P3P user-agent may not give away the MIME type or browser type in a request for a reference file because the request is in the safe zone.

This means that a combination of the two methods might be best—if you know that the request comes from the legacy Internet, you know that the application will not ask for the location ever, so you can send a reference file pointing to the simpler policy file(s). If the request comes from a mobile Internet browser, or if you cannot tell where it comes from, you state that you will need the location and what you will do with it.

Creating a Policy File

From the first sections of this chapter, you could see that there will be new kinds of data within a mobile Internet environment. There are mainly three kinds of new information:

- The geographical location of the user
- The user-agent profile
- User profiles consisting of the following:
  - Preferences that refer to customizations that the user made—like the desire to receive images
  - User-entered information like name and address

You may not need all the information that is within the user-agent profile every time, or you may reuse parts of it. In 2001, we created a suggested vocabulary, described in Appendix B, for WAP user-agents. The vocabulary is not complete because it was created for WAP 1.2.1, but it can easily be modified to fit new WAP versions.

An example policy using this schema is presented together with the schema that follows:

```
<DATASCHEMA xmlns="http://www.w3.org/2000/12/P3Pv1">
  <DATA-STRUCT name="uaprof.HardwarePlatform.BluetoothProfile"
    short-description="Supported Bluetooth profiles as defined in the
Bluetooth specification [BLT]">
  </DATA-STRUCT>
  <DATA-STRUCT name="uaprof.HardwarePlatform.BitsPerPixel"
    short-description="The number of bits of color or grayscale information
per pixel">
  </DATA-STRUCT>
  <DATA-STRUCT name="uaprof.HardwarePlatform.ColorCapable"
    short-description="Whether the device display supports color">
  </DATA-STRUCT>
  <DATA-STRUCT name="uaprof.HardwarePlatform.CPU"
    short-description="Name and model number of device CPU">
  </DATA-STRUCT>
  <DATA-STRUCT name="uaprof.HardwarePlatform.ImageCapable"
    short-description="Whether the device supports the display of images">
```

```
  </DATA-STRUCT>
  <DATA-STRUCT name="uaprof.HardwarePlatform.InputCharSet"
    short-description="List of character sets supported by the device for
text entry">
  </DATA-STRUCT>
  <DATA-STRUCT name="uaprof.HardwarePlatform.Keyboard"
    short-description="Type of keyboard supported by the device">
  </DATA-STRUCT>
  <DATA-STRUCT name="uaprof.HardwarePlatform.Model"
    short-description="Model number assigned to the terminal device by the
vendor or manufacturer">
  </DATA-STRUCT>
  <DATA-STRUCT name="uaprof.HardwarePlatform.NumberOfSoftKeys"
    short-description="Number of soft keys available on the device">
  </DATA-STRUCT>
  <DATA-STRUCT name="uaprof.HardwarePlatform.OutputCharSet"
    short-description="List of character sets supported by the device for
output to the display">
  </DATA-STRUCT>
  <DATA-STRUCT name="uaprof.HardwarePlatform.PixelAspectRatio"
    short-description="Ratio of pixel width to pixel height">
  </DATA-STRUCT>
  <DATA-STRUCT name="uaprof.HardwarePlatform.PointingResolution"
    short-description="Type of resolution of the pointing accessory
supported by the device">
  </DATA-STRUCT>
  <DATA-STRUCT name="uaprof.HardwarePlatform.ScreenSize"
    short-description="The size of the device's screen in units of pixels">
  </DATA-STRUCT>
  <DATA-STRUCT name="uaprof.HardwarePlatform.ScreenSizeChar"
    short-description="Size of the device's screen in units of characters.
(Number of characters per row)x(Number of rows). In calculating this
attribute use the largest character in the device's default font.">
  </DATA-STRUCT>
  <DATA-STRUCT name="uaprof.HardwarePlatform.SoundOutputCapable"
    short-description="Indicates whether the device supports sound output">
  </DATA-STRUCT>
  <DATA-STRUCT name="uaprof.HardwarePlatform.StandardFontProportional"
    short-description="Indicates whether the device's standard font is
proportional">
  </DATA-STRUCT>
  <DATA-STRUCT name="uaprof.HardwarePlatform.TextInputCapable"
    short-description="Indicates whether the device supports alpha-numeric
text entry">
  </DATA-STRUCT>
```

```
<DATA-STRUCT name="uaprof.HardwarePlatform.Vendor"
  short-description="Name of the vendor manufacturing the terminal
device">
</DATA-STRUCT>
<DATA-STRUCT name="uaprof.HardwarePlatform.VoiceInputCapable"
  short-description="Indicates whether the device supports any form of
voice input, including speech recognition">
</DATA-STRUCT>

<DATA-STRUCT name="uaprof.SoftwarePlatform.AcceptDownloadableSoftware"
  short-description="Indicates the user's preference on whether to
accept
downloadable software">
</DATA-STRUCT>
<DATA-STRUCT name="uaprof.SoftwarePlatform.AudioInputEncoder"
  short-description="List of audio input encoders supported by the
device">
</DATA-STRUCT>
<DATA-STRUCT name="uaprof.SoftwarePlatform.CcppAccept"
  short-description="List of content types the device supports">
</DATA-STRUCT>
<DATA-STRUCT name="uaprof.SoftwarePlatform.CcppAccept-Charset"
  short-description="List of character sets the device supports">
</DATA-STRUCT>
<DATA-STRUCT name="uaprof.SoftwarePlatform.CcppAccept-Encoding"
  short-description="List of transfer encodings the device supports">
</DATA-STRUCT>
<DATA-STRUCT name="uaprof.SoftwarePlatform.CcppAccept-Language"
  short-description="List of preferred document languages">
</DATA-STRUCT>
<DATA-STRUCT name="uaprof.SoftwarePlatform.DownloadableSoftwareSupport"
  short-description="List of executable content types which the device
supports and which it is willing to accept from the network">
</DATA-STRUCT>
<DATA-STRUCT name="uaprof.SoftwarePlatform.JavaEnabled"
  short-description="Indicates whether the device supports a Java virtual
machine">
</DATA-STRUCT>
<DATA-STRUCT name="uaprof.SoftwarePlatform.JavaPlatform"
  short-description="The list of JAVA platforms and profiles installed in
the device.">
</DATA-STRUCT>
<DATA-STRUCT name="uaprof.SoftwarePlatform.JVMVersion"
  short-description="List of the Java virtual machines installed on the
device">
```

```
  </DATA-STRUCT>
  <DATA-STRUCT name="uaprof.SoftwarePlatform.MexeSpec"
    short-description="Class mark specialization">
  </DATA-STRUCT>
  <DATA-STRUCT name="uaprof.SoftwarePlatform.MexeClassmarks"
    short-description="List of MExE classmarks supported by the device.">
  </DATA-STRUCT>
  <DATA-STRUCT name="uaprof.SoftwarePlatform.MexeSecureDomains"
    short-description="Indicates whether the device supports MExE security
domains as specified in the MExE specifications">
  </DATA-STRUCT>
  <DATA-STRUCT name="uaprof.SoftwarePlatform.OSName"
    short-description="Name of the device's operating system">
  </DATA-STRUCT>
  <DATA-STRUCT name="uaprof.SoftwarePlatform.OSVendor"
    short-description="Vendor of the device's operating system">
  </DATA-STRUCT>
  <DATA-STRUCT name="uaprof.SoftwarePlatform.OSVersion"
    short-description="Version of the device's operating system">
  </DATA-STRUCT>
  <DATA-STRUCT name="uaprof.SoftwarePlatform.RecipientAppAgent"
    short-description="User agent associated with the current request">
  </DATA-STRUCT>
  <DATA-STRUCT name="uaprof.SoftwarePlatform.SoftwareNumber"
    short-description="Version of the device-specific software
(firmware) to
which the device's low-level software conforms">
  </DATA-STRUCT>
  <DATA-STRUCT name="uaprof.SoftwarePlatform.VideoInputEncoder"
    short-description="List of video input encoders supported by the
device">
  </DATA-STRUCT>

  <DATA-STRUCT name="uaprof.NetworkCharacteristics.CurrentBearerService"
    short-description="The bearer on which the current session was
opened">
  </DATA-STRUCT>
  <DATA-STRUCT name="uaprof.NetworkCharacteristics.SecuritySupport"
    short-description="List of types of security or encryption mechanisms
supported by the device.">
  </DATA-STRUCT>
  <DATA-STRUCT name="uaprof.NetworkCharacteristics.SupportedBearers"
    short-description="List of bearers supported by the device">
  </DATA-STRUCT>
  <DATA-STRUCT
```

```
name="uaprof.NetworkCharacteristics.SupportedBluetoothVersion"
    short-description="Supported Bluetooth version">
  </DATA-STRUCT>

  <DATA-STRUCT name="uaprof.BrowserUA.BrowserName"
    short-description="Name of the browser user agent associated with the
current request">
  </DATA-STRUCT>
  <DATA-STRUCT name="uaprof.BrowserUA.BrowserVersion"
    short-description="Version of the browser">
  </DATA-STRUCT>
  <DATA-STRUCT name="uaprof.BrowserUA.DownloadableBrowserApps"
    short-description="List of executable content types which the browser
supports and which it is willing to accept from the network">
  </DATA-STRUCT>
  <DATA-STRUCT name="uaprof.BrowserUA.FramesCapable"
    short-description="Indicates whether the browser is capable of
displaying frames">
  </DATA-STRUCT>
  <DATA-STRUCT name="uaprof.BrowserUA.HtmlVersion"
    short-description="Version of HyperText Markup Language (HTML) sup-
ported
by the browser">
  </DATA-STRUCT>
  <DATA-STRUCT name="uaprof.BrowserUA.JavaAppletEnabled"
    short-description="Indicates whether the browser supports Java
applets">
  </DATA-STRUCT>
  <DATA-STRUCT name="uaprof.BrowserUA.JavaScriptEnabled"
    short-description="Indicates whether the browser supports
JavaScript">
  </DATA-STRUCT>
  <DATA-STRUCT name="uaprof.BrowserUA.JavaScriptVersion"
    short-description="Version of the JavaScript language supported by the
browser">
  </DATA-STRUCT>
  <DATA-STRUCT name="uaprof.BrowserUA.PreferenceForFrames"
    short-description="Indicates the user's preference for receiving HTML
content that contains frames">
  </DATA-STRUCT>
  <DATA-STRUCT name="uaprof.BrowserUA.TablesCapable"
    short-description="Indicates whether the browser is capable of
displaying tables">
  </DATA-STRUCT>
  <DATA-STRUCT name="uaprof.BrowserUA.XhtmlVersion"
    short-description="Version of XHTML supported by the browser">
```

```
  </DATA-STRUCT>

  <DATA-STRUCT name="uaprof.WapCharacteristics.SupportedPictogramSet"
    short-description="Pictogram classes supported by the device as
defined
in the WAP Pictogram specification">
  </DATA-STRUCT>
  <DATA-STRUCT name="uaprof.WapCharacteristics.WapDeviceClass"
    short-description="Classification of the device based on capabili-
ties as
identified in the WAP 1.1 specifications">
  </DATA-STRUCT>
  <DATA-STRUCT name="uaprof.WapCharacteristics.WapVersion"
    short-description="Version of WAP supported">
  </DATA-STRUCT>
  <DATA-STRUCT name="uaprof.WapCharacteristics.WmlDeckSize"
    short-description="Maximum size of a WML deck that can be downloaded to
the device">
  </DATA-STRUCT>
  <DATA-STRUCT name="uaprof.WapCharacteristics.WmlScriptLibraries"
    short-description="List of mandatory and optional libraries sup-
ported in
the device's WMLScript VM">
  </DATA-STRUCT>
  <DATA-STRUCT name="uaprof.WapCharacteristics.WmlScriptVersion"
    short-description="List of WMLScript versions supported by the
device">
  </DATA-STRUCT>
  <DATA-STRUCT name="uaprof.WapCharacteristics.WmlVersion"
    short-description="List of WML language versions supported by the
device">
  </DATA-STRUCT>
  <DATA-STRUCT name="uaprof.WapCharacteristics.WtaiLibraries"
    short-description="List of WTAI network common and network specific
libraries supported by the device">
  </DATA-STRUCT>
  <DATA-STRUCT name="uaprof.WapCharacteristics.WtaVersion"
    short-description="Version of WTA user agent">
  </DATA-STRUCT>

  <DATA-STRUCT name="uaprof.PushCharacteristics.Push-Accept"
    short-description="List of content types the device supports for
push">
  </DATA-STRUCT>
  <DATA-STRUCT name="uaprof.PushCharacteristics.Push-Accept-Charset"
    short-description="List of character sets the device supports for
push">
  </DATA-STRUCT>
  <DATA-STRUCT name="uaprof.PushCharacteristics.Push-Accept-Encoding"
```

```
    short-description="List of transfer encodings the device supports for
push">
  </DATA-STRUCT>
  <DATA-STRUCT name="uaprof.PushCharacteristics.Push-Accept-Language"
    short-description="List of preferred document languages for push">
  </DATA-STRUCT>
  <DATA-STRUCT name="uaprof.PushCharacteristics.Push-Accept-AppID"
    short-description="List of applications the device supports for push">
  </DATA-STRUCT>
  <DATA-STRUCT name="uaprof.PushCharacteristics.Push-MsgSize"
    short-description="Maximum size in bytes of a push message that the
device can handle">
  </DATA-STRUCT>
  <DATA-STRUCT name="uaprof.PushCharacteristics.Push-MaxPushReq"
    short-description="Maximum number of outstanding push requests that the
device can handle">
  </DATA-STRUCT>
</DATASCHEMA>

<POLICIES xmlns="http://www.w3.org/2002/01/P3Pv1">
 <POLICY name="default"
     discuri="http://www.werespectyou.com/privacy/policy.html"
     opturi="http://www.werespectyou.com/preferences.html"
     xml:lang="en">
<ENTITY>
   <DATA-GROUP>
    <DATA ref="#business.name">WeRespectYou</DATA>
    <DATA ref="#business.contact-info.postal.street">42, Web
Street</DATA>
    <DATA ref="#business.contact-info.postal.city">Gotham City</DATA>
    <DATA ref="#business.contact-info.postal.stateprov">AA</DATA>
    <DATA ref="#business.contact-info.postal.postalcode">12345</DATA>
    <DATA ref="#business.contact-info.postal.country">USA</DATA>
    <DATA ref="#business.contact-info.online.email">privacy@werespec-
tyou.com</DATA>
    <DATA ref="#business.contact-
info.telecom.telephone.intcode">1</DATA>
    <DATA ref="#business.contact-
info.telecom.telephone.loccode">555</DATA>
    <DATA ref="#business.contact-info.telecom.telephone.num-
ber">123456</DATA>
   </DATA-GROUP>
 </ENTITY>
 <ACCESS><nonident/></ACCESS>
 <DISPUTES-GROUP>
  <DISPUTES resolution-type="independent"
    service="http://www.thirdparty.org">
```

```
    <REMEDIES><correct/></REMEDIES>
   </DISPUTES>
  </DISPUTES-GROUP>
  <STATEMENT>
   <PURPOSE<current/></PURPOSE>
   <RECIPIENT><ours/></RECIPIENT>
   <RETENTION><no-retention/></RETENTION>
   <DATA-GROUP>
    <DATA ref="#dynamic.clickstream"/>
    <DATA ref="#dynamic.http"/>
   </DATA-GROUP>
  </STATEMENT>
 <STATEMENT>
      <CONSEQUENCE>
              We use this information to customize the Web site to fit
your device.
      </CONSEQUENCE>
      <PURPOSE>
              <current/>
      </PURPOSE>
      <RECIPIENT>
              <ours/>
      </RECIPIENT>
      <RETENTION>
              <no-retention/>
      </RETENTION>
      <DATA-GROUP>
              <DATA ref="#uaprof.HardwarePlatform.BluetoothProfile"
optional="yes"><CATEGORIES><computer/></CATEGORIES></DATA>
              <DATA ref="#uaprof.HardwarePlatform.BitsPerPixel"
optional="yes"><CATEGORIES><computer/></CATEGORIES></DATA>
              <DATA ref="#uaprof.HardwarePlatform.ColorCapable"
optional="yes"><CATEGORIES><computer/></CATEGORIES></DATA>
              <DATA ref="#uaprof.HardwarePlatform.CPU"
optional="yes"><CATEGORIES><computer/></CATEGORIES></DATA>
              <DATA ref="#uaprof.HardwarePlatform.ImageCapable"
optional="yes"><CATEGORIES><computer/></CATEGORIES></DATA>
              <DATA ref="#uaprof.HardwarePlatform.InputCharSet"
optional="yes"><CATEGORIES><computer/></CATEGORIES></DATA>
              <DATA ref="#uaprof.HardwarePlatform.Keyboard"
optional="yes"><CATEGORIES><computer/></CATEGORIES></DATA>
              <DATA ref="#uaprof.HardwarePlatform.Model"
optional="yes"><CATEGORIES><computer/></CATEGORIES></DATA>
              <DATA ref="#uaprof.HardwarePlatform.NumberOfSoftKeys"
optional="yes"><CATEGORIES><computer/></CATEGORIES></DATA>
              <DATA ref="#uaprof.HardwarePlatform.OutputCharSet"
optional="yes"><CATEGORIES><computer/></CATEGORIES></DATA>
              <DATA ref="#uaprof.HardwarePlatform.PixelAspectRatio"
optional="yes"><CATEGORIES><computer/></CATEGORIES></DATA>
              <DATA ref="#uaprof.HardwarePlatform.PointingResolution"
```

```
optional="yes"><CATEGORIES><computer/></CATEGORIES></DATA>
              <DATA ref="#uaprof.HardwarePlatform.ScreenSize"
optional="yes"><CATEGORIES><computer/></CATEGORIES></DATA>
              <DATA ref="#uaprof.HardwarePlatform.ScreenSizeChar"
optional="yes"><CATEGORIES><computer/></CATEGORIES></DATA>
              <DATA ref="#uaprof.HardwarePlatform.SoundOutputCapable"
optional="yes"><CATEGORIES><computer/></CATEGORIES></DATA>
              <DATA
ref="#uaprof.HardwarePlatform.StandardFontProportional"
optional="yes"><CATEGORIES><computer/></CATEGORIES></DATA>
              <DATA ref="#uaprof.HardwarePlatform.TextInputCapable"
optional="yes"><CATEGORIES><computer/></CATEGORIES></DATA>
              <DATA ref="#uaprof.HardwarePlatform.Vendor"
optional="yes"><CATEGORIES><computer/></CATEGORIES></DATA>
              <DATA ref="#uaprof.HardwarePlatform.VoiceInputCapable"
optional="yes"><CATEGORIES><computer/></CATEGORIES></DATA>
              <DATA
ref="#uaprof.SoftwarePlatform.AcceptDownloadableSoftware"
optional="yes"><CATEGORIES><computer/></CATEGORIES></DATA>
              <DATA ref="#uaprof.SoftwarePlatform.AudioInputEncoder"
optional="yes"><CATEGORIES><computer/></CATEGORIES></DATA>
              <DATA ref="#uaprof.SoftwarePlatform.CcppAccept"
optional="yes"><CATEGORIES><computer/></CATEGORIES></DATA>
              <DATA ref="#uaprof.SoftwarePlatform.CcppAccept-Charset"
optional="yes"><CATEGORIES><computer/></CATEGORIES></DATA>
              <DATA ref="#uaprof.SoftwarePlatform.CcppAccept-Encoding"
optional="yes"><CATEGORIES><computer/></CATEGORIES></DATA>
              <DATA ref="#uaprof.SoftwarePlatform.CcppAccept-Language"
optional="yes"><CATEGORIES><computer/></CATEGORIES></DATA>
              <DATA
ref="#uaprof.SoftwarePlatform.DownloadableSoftwareSupport"
optional="yes"><CATEGORIES><computer/></CATEGORIES></DATA>
              <DATA ref="#uaprof.SoftwarePlatform.JavaEnabled"
optional="yes"><CATEGORIES><computer/></CATEGORIES></DATA>
              <DATA ref="#uaprof.SoftwarePlatform.JavaPlatform"
optional="yes"><CATEGORIES><computer/></CATEGORIES></DATA>
              <DATA ref="#uaprof.SoftwarePlatform.JVMVersion"
optional="yes"><CATEGORIES><computer/></CATEGORIES></DATA>
              <DATA ref="#uaprof.SoftwarePlatform.MexeSpec"
optional="yes"><CATEGORIES><computer/></CATEGORIES></DATA>
              <DATA ref="#uaprof.SoftwarePlatform.MexeClassmarks"
optional="yes"><CATEGORIES><computer/></CATEGORIES></DATA>
              <DATA ref="#uaprof.SoftwarePlatform.MexeSecureDomains"
optional="yes"><CATEGORIES><computer/></CATEGORIES></DATA>
              <DATA ref="#uaprof.SoftwarePlatform.OSName"
optional="yes"><CATEGORIES><computer/></CATEGORIES></DATA>
              <DATA ref="#uaprof.SoftwarePlatform.OSVendor"
optional="yes"><CATEGORIES><computer/></CATEGORIES></DATA>
              <DATA ref="#uaprof.SoftwarePlatform.OSVersion"
optional="yes"><CATEGORIES><computer/></CATEGORIES></DATA>
```

```
            <DATA ref="#uaprof.SoftwarePlatform.RecipientAppAgent"
optional="yes"><CATEGORIES><computer/></CATEGORIES></DATA>
            <DATA ref="#uaprof.SoftwarePlatform.SoftwareNumber"
optional="yes"><CATEGORIES><computer/></CATEGORIES></DATA>
            <DATA ref="#uaprof.SoftwarePlatform.VideoInputEncoder"
optional="yes"><CATEGORIES><computer/></CATEGORIES></DATA>
            <DATA
ref="#uaprof.NetworkCharacteristics.CurrentBearerService"
optional="yes"><CATEGORIES><computer/></CATEGORIES></DATA>
            <DATA ref="#uaprof.NetworkCharacteristics.SecuritySupport"
optional="yes"><CATEGORIES><computer/></CATEGORIES></DATA>
            <DATA ref="#uaprof.NetworkCharacteristics.SupportedBearers"
optional="yes"><CATEGORIES><computer/></CATEGORIES></DATA>
            <DATA
ref="#uaprof.NetworkCharacteristics.SupportedBluetoothVersion"
optional="yes"><CATEGORIES><computer/></CATEGORIES></DATA>
            <DATA ref="#uaprof.BrowserUA.BrowserName"
optional="yes"><CATEGORIES><computer/></CATEGORIES></DATA>
            <DATA ref="#uaprof.BrowserUA.BrowserVersion"
optional="yes"><CATEGORIES><computer/></CATEGORIES></DATA>
            <DATA ref="#uaprof.BrowserUA.DownloadableBrowserApps"
optional="yes"><CATEGORIES><computer/></CATEGORIES></DATA>
            <DATA ref="#uaprof.BrowserUA.FramesCapable"
optional="yes"><CATEGORIES><computer/></CATEGORIES></DATA>
            <DATA ref="#uaprof.BrowserUA.HtmlVersion"
optional="yes"><CATEGORIES><computer/></CATEGORIES></DATA>
            <DATA ref="#uaprof.BrowserUA.JavaAppletEnabled"
optional="yes"><CATEGORIES><computer/></CATEGORIES></DATA>
            <DATA ref="#uaprof.BrowserUA.JavaScriptEnabled"
optional="yes"><CATEGORIES><computer/></CATEGORIES></DATA>
            <DATA ref="#uaprof.BrowserUA.JavaScriptVersion"
optional="yes"><CATEGORIES><computer/></CATEGORIES></DATA>
            <DATA ref="#uaprof.BrowserUA.PreferenceForFrames"
optional="yes"><CATEGORIES><computer/></CATEGORIES></DATA>
            <DATA ref="#uaprof.BrowserUA.TablesCapable"
optional="yes"><CATEGORIES><computer/></CATEGORIES></DATA>
            <DATA ref="#uaprof.BrowserUA.XhtmlVersion"
optional="yes"><CATEGORIES><computer/></CATEGORIES></DATA>
            <DATA ref="#uaprof.WapCharacteristics.SupportedPictogramSet"
optional="yes"><CATEGORIES><computer/></CATEGORIES></DATA>
            <DATA ref="#uaprof.WapCharacteristics.WapDeviceClass"
optional="yes"><CATEGORIES><computer/></CATEGORIES></DATA>
            <DATA ref="#uaprof.WapCharacteristics.WapVersion"
optional="yes"><CATEGORIES><computer/></CATEGORIES></DATA>
            <DATA ref="#uaprof.WapCharacteristics.WmlDeckSize"
optional="yes"><CATEGORIES><computer/></CATEGORIES></DATA>
            <DATA ref="#uaprof.WapCharacteristics.WmlScriptLibraries"
optional="yes"><CATEGORIES><computer/></CATEGORIES></DATA>
            <DATA ref="#uaprof.WapCharacteristics.WmlScriptVersion"
```

```
optional="yes"><CATEGORIES><computer/></CATEGORIES></DATA>
              <DATA ref="#uaprof.WapCharacteristics.WmlVersion"
optional="yes"><CATEGORIES><computer/></CATEGORIES></DATA>
              <DATA ref="#uaprof.WapCharacteristics.WtaiLibraries"
optional="yes"><CATEGORIES><computer/></CATEGORIES></DATA>
              <DATA ref="#uaprof.WapCharacteristics.WtaVersion"
optional="yes"><CATEGORIES><computer/></CATEGORIES></DATA>
              <DATA ref="#uaprof.PushCharacteristics.Push-Accept"
optional="yes"><CATEGORIES><computer/></CATEGORIES></DATA>
              <DATA ref="#uaprof.PushCharacteristics.Push-Accept-Charset"
optional="yes"><CATEGORIES><computer/></CATEGORIES></DATA>
              <DATA ref="#uaprof.PushCharacteristics.Push-Accept-Encoding"
optional="yes"><CATEGORIES><computer/></CATEGORIES></DATA>
              <DATA ref="#uaprof.PushCharacteristics.Push-Accept-Language"
optional="yes"><CATEGORIES><computer/></CATEGORIES></DATA>
              <DATA ref="#uaprof.PushCharacteristics.Push-Accept-AppID"
optional="yes"><CATEGORIES><computer/></CATEGORIES></DATA>
              <DATA ref="#uaprof.PushCharacteristics.Push-MsgSize"
optional="yes"><CATEGORIES><computer/></CATEGORIES></DATA>
              <DATA ref="#uaprof.PushCharacteristics.Push-MaxPushReq"
optional="yes"><CATEGORIES><computer/></CATEGORIES></DATA>
      </DATA-GROUP>
</STATEMENT>
</POLICY>
</POLICIES>
```

You will not need to do all this. Probably, you will use a couple of elements from the user-agent profile—for example, #uaprof.HardwarePlatform.ScreenSize and #uaprof.HardwarePlatform.ColorCapable. These could be processed to present the user with the best possible layout and possibly store it for some reason.

Profile Data Conveyance and Cookie-Policy Receipts

In Chapter 11 we discussed how personal data can be transmitted using P3P as a method to request data and not only state what will be done when the data is transmitted. This method is particularly interesting in mobile Internet environments, due to their limited input and output capabilities, as described at the beginning of this chapter.

User-agent profiles, together with user profiles, can be conveyed in HTTP headers using CC/PP or UAProf .

Imagine the following scenario:

- Greta wants as little information as possible to be conveyed about her when she uses mobile Internet.
- She goes to wap.werespectyou.com. In its default policy, the site requests her screen size and wants to know if her device is image capable. It also wants to place a cookie.
- Her device, or her user-agent at the operator's premises, or her user-agent at her PC at home or within her intranet will parse the policy, check it against her preferences, ask her if necessary, and then convey the screen size and image capabilities. It will also return a cookie-policy receipt, indicating that the cookie policy was read and understood and that it is OK to place a cookie.
- After surfing for a while, she wants to create a user account. The site where she is supposed to enter her name, address, and other personal data has a different policy. When her user-agent has parsed this policy, it creates a CC/PP profile, as in Chapter 11, and sends it with the request.
- The responding application at werespectyou.com is thrilled to discover that all the data is already there with the request, and it returns a page saying that "this is what you entered, create account?"
- Greta presses yes, and that completes the use case.

She gained convenience. She also gained privacy because a contract was established with the site; if this contract is broken, she will be able to go to court.

This use case pretty much completes all the examples that we have discussed in this book—P3P today, the future of P3P, what it is, and what it is not. If used improperly, P3P is a lot of overhead for programmers and generates unnecessary traffic on the Internet. If used properly, it is a powerful tool to make users and servers agree with a minimum of communication.

We would like to conclude as we began, by quoting Alan Westin from 1967:

> *"Privacy is the claim of individuals to determine how, when, and to what extent information about them is communicated to others."*

Additional Reading

`http://www.w3.org/P3P`	The P3P site
`http://www.w3.org/TR/CCPP-trust/`	CC/PP Implementor's Guide: Privacy and Protocols
`http://www.w3.org/TR/CCPP-struct-vocab/`	Composite Capability/Preference Profiles (CC/PP): Structure and Vocabularies
`http://www.openmobilealliance.org/`	Open Mobile Alliance
Designing Wireless Application Services	Wiley, Johan Hjelm

An XML Tutorial

The aim of this appendix is to give a basic introduction to eXtensible Markup Language (XML). Note, however, that this description is not exhaustive, and therefore it gives only a brief orientation to the sometimes complex world of XML. We explain the concepts of XML schemas in Appendix B.

Background

XML is a universal format for structuring documents and data primarily for the Web. It was first released as a W3C recommendation in February 1998, and the base specification is referred to as XML 1.0. A second edition of this specification was announced in October 2000. The following design goals are expressed in the specification (see Extensible Markup Language (XML) 1.0, 2nd edition, W3C Recommendation 6 October 2000, http://www.w3.org/TR/2000/REC-cml-20001006):

1. XML shall be straightforwardly usable over the Internet.
2. XML shall support a wide variety of applications.
3. XML shall be compatible with SGML.
4. It shall be easy to write programs, which process XML documents.
5. The number of optional features in XML is to be kept to the absolute minimum, ideally zero.

6. XML documents should be human legible and reasonably clear.
7. The XML design should be prepared quickly.
8. The design of XML shall be formal and concise.
9. XML documents shall be easy to create.
10. Terseness in XML markup is of minimal importance.

XML is essentially derived from the Standard Generalized Markup Language (SGML), which was developed in the early 1980s. SGML is a very flexible and powerful meta-language. A meta-language is a language that is used for defining markup languages. In 1986, SGML became an ISO standard (ISO 8879). At that time, SGML was used in very large documentation projects, especially for technical documentation.

General XML Concepts

XML is both a so-called meta-language and a markup language in its own right.[1] A meta-language is a language used to specify new markup languages for documents containing structured information. Two examples of markup languages specified using XML are Wireless Markup Language (WML) and eXtensible HyperText Markup Language (XHTML). The latter is the successor to HyperText Markup Language (HTML). A markup language, on the other hand, is a language in which syntactically delimited characters can be added to the data of a document to represent a certain structure. Probably the most common form of markup in XML is the tag, which is introduced in the following section. Another example is Processing Instructions (PIs), which are described later in the chapter.

As mentioned previously, XML is designed to make it easy to exchange structured information over the Internet. XML is a low-level syntax for representing structured data. We could also think of XML as a set of rules for designing text formats that let you structure your information.

Tags and Attributes

XML, as well as HTML, makes use of tags for structuring information. An XML document consists of a set of tags, referred to as a *tag set*, which encapsulates the content of the document. Tags are words bracketed by

[1]Some people are, however, of the opinion that XML is just a meta-language. For example, Johan Hjelm argues that point in *Designing Wireless Information Services*, which is listed in some Additional Reading sections of the book.

< and >, and they are most often pairs. Hence, there is a start tag and an end tag, and everything between these two is content. In XML, there is actually a rule that says that all tags must be paired. To be a bit more concrete, one entry taken from a fictitious address book formatted with XML is given here.

```
<adressbook>
     <addressbookentry>
          <firstname>Sherlock</firstname>
          <lastname>Holmes</lastname>
          <address country="UK">
               <street>Baker street 221b</street>
               <city>London</city>
          </address>
     </addressbookentry>
</addressbook>
```

This simple example shows numerous syntactical features of XML. First of all, seven different tag pairs are used in this example—for instance, <firstname> and </firstname>.

XML is case sensitive, wheras HTML is not.

Another important concept in the XML terminology is *element*. This is the piece of information encapsulated by a start tag and an end tag. Hence, <city>London</city> from the example is an example of a simple element.

From the example, we can see that elements can be nested. For example, the element starting with the tag <firstname> is part of the address book entry element. Elements must, however, be perfectly nested within one other. This means that <head><title>My Title</head> </title> is syntactically incorrect, but <head><title>My Title </title></head> is correct.

An element in XML may be further enriched by an attribute. An attribute is of the form: name="value". This implies that an attribute in XML provides additional information about elements, and they often provide information that is not part of the data. The address element in the preceding example has an attribute (country="UK") that specifies which country this particular address is in.

XML also allows so-called empty tags. No empty tags are used in the example. The concept, though, is simple. Assume an element (for example, network) with no content, but with an attribute (for example, name="CISCO"). Such an element can be specified in an XML document in the following two ways:

1. <network name="CISCO"></network>
2. <network name="CISCO"/>

The latter is the empty tag because there is no end tag. Empty tags can be used only in cases when there is no content involved.

Document Type Definition (DTD)

Document Type Definition (DTD) is another important concept in XML. All valid XML documents must have an associated DTD. Most users of XML will indeed never write a DTD by themselves. Instead, they will use a predefined one.

What is a DTD then? A DTD is mainly used to do the following:

- Define the set of possible tags.
- Define the set of attributes that either must be used or could be used in relation with the tags.
- Specify structural relationships between tags. For example, the <city> tag in the preceding example may appear within an <address>, but not the other way around.
- Specify the sequence of tags, if any. For example, assume a DTD used to create a book. In a book, one could optionally use a <preface> tag. If such a tag is used, it must appear before the first <chapter> tag.

In summary, we could say that the DTD tells XML applications how to interpret the content of the document—that is, it is a grammar for the document. The DTD for the address book example introduced in the previous subsection follows. Note that the line numbers to the left have been added for easier references in the description that follows.

```
0. <!-- Address book Data Type Definition (DTD) -->
1. <!ELEMENT addressbook          (addressbookentry*)>
2. <!ELEMENT addressbookentry     (firstname, lastname, address)>
3. <!ELEMENT firstname            (#PCDATA)>
4. <!ELEMENT lastname             (#PCDATA)>
5. <!ELEMENT address              (city, street)>
6. <!ATTLIST address
7.         country                CDATA #REQUIRED>
8. <!ELEMENT city                (#PCDATA)>
9. <!ELEMENT street              (#PCDATA)>
```

Each line of the DTD is described in the following:

- Line 0 is just a descriptive comment about what is coming next. A comment in XML starts with "<!—" and ends with "—>".
- Line 1 indicates that there is an address book that contains zero or more entries. This element is the so-called root element in the example. A root element is the starting point for an XML parser, and it encapsulates all the other tags.
- Line 2 specifies that an address book entry consist of three parts: first name, second name, and an address.
- Lines 3 and 4 define data; both first and second name consist of parsed character data. Parsed character data (#PCDATA) is plain text, which a parser must read through completely before making any processing, such as collapsing whitespace.
- Line 5 specifies that an address, in this case, consists of a city and a street.
- Lines 6 and 7 together tell data that the address tag must have an attribute country. This attribute contains nonparsed character data or simply character data (CDATA for short), which means that no processing should be performed on the data.
- Lines 8 and 9, finally, specify that data for city as well as street consists of parsed character data.

Prolog

The first few lines of an XML document are most often a prolog.

NOTE

It is optional, but advised, that each XML document has a prolog.

A prolog may consist of two optional parts. The first part is a line that identifies which version of XML, encoding information, and other such elements are being used. A simple specification could be as follows:

```
<?xml version="1.0"?>
```

This declaration could be enhanced with encoding information and information about whether this document could be processed separately.

The second part of the prolog is the document type declaration, which is different from DTD. The document type declaration indicates where the grammar (that is, the DTD) resides. An example of such a declaration follows.

```
<!DOCTYPE  address-book>
```

Remember that <address-book> is the root element in our example. If an external DTD (address-book.dtd) is used instead, which is stored at http://www.werespectyou.com, the declaration will be as follows:

```
<!DOCTYPE address-book SYSTEM http://www.werespectyou.com/address-book.dtd>
```

The pointer to an external DTD consists of two parts—the keyword SYSTEM, followed by a Universal Resource Identifier (URI) that indicates where the DTD is actually located. The URI in this particular case is http://www.werespectyou.com/address-book.dtd. A URI is, for all practical purposes, identical in appearance and function to a Uniform Resource Locator (URL), which was introduced in Chapter 3.

Processing Instructions

Processing Instructions (PIs) are used in situations where an XML document has to prepare the application to handle special sorts of content that are not covered by conventions in XML or to perform a non-XML function. We have indeed already seen a PI—the XML declaration, with XML version identification, which was described previously. Another example is this:

```
<?mp3 version="2.5" frequency="44.1kHz" bitrate="128Kbps"?>
```

This information might be extremely useful for an XML-aware browser that is expected to handle Mp3 files. Version number, frequency response, and the bit rate at which the music was recorded are specified in the preceding PI.

Namespaces

The XML namespaces recommendation provides a way to distinguish between duplicate element type and attribute names. Duplicates may occur when element type and attribute names from two different DTDs are used within a single document.

What is an XML namespace? Simply speaking, it is nothing but a collection of element types and attribute names. Each namespace can further be identified by a unique name, which is a URI. An element type or attribute name in a namespace is uniquely identified with a two-part name—the name of the namespace and its local name. An xmlns attribute is used when declaring a namespace in XML. An example of a namespace declaration is as follows:

```
<werespectyou:A xmlns:werespectyou="http://www.werespectyou.com" >
<werespectyou:B>ABCD</werespectyou:B>
<C>EFGH</C>
</werespectyou:A>
```

In the example, element type name A and B are in the `http://www.werespectyou.com` namespace, which is associated with the werespectyou prefix. Element type name C, on the other hand, is not in any XML namespaces at all.

In summary, the two-part naming system is the only thing defined by the XML namespaces recommendation, which is in the list of additional reading at the end of this book.

Other Related Recommendations

As already mentioned, the XML 1.0 recommendation specifies the syntax of XML, which is how the elements and attributes should be defined. XML namespaces, described previously, are defined in another recommendation (see *Additional Reading* later in this appendix). Several more related specifications are also available at `http://www.w3.org`, and a few of them are briefly described here.

- *XML Schema* defines how the tags should be handled. The W3C consortium is working on a new 1.1 specification. XML Schema is further described in Appendix B.
- *XSL (eXtensible Stylesheet Language)* is a language for expressing style sheets. A style sheet is a file that describes how to display an XML document of a given type. See http://www.w3.org/Style/XSL/ for more information on this topic.
- *XSLT (XSL Transformations)* is a language for transforming XML documents into other XML documents. XSLT is designed for use as part of XSL. The W3C recommendation for XSLT can be found at `http://www.w3.org/TR/xslt`.

- *XLink (XML Linking Language)* allows elements to be inserted into XML documents in order to create and describe links between resources. See `http://www.w3.org/XML/Linking` for more details.
- *XPointer (XML Pointer Language)* is another language to be used as a fragment identifier for any URI reference that locates a resource of Internet media type text/xml or application/xml. See `http://www.w3.org/XML/Linking` for further details.
- *XPath (XML Path Language)* is yet another language for addressing parts of an XML document, designed to be used by both XSLT and XPointer. The W3C recommendation for XPath can be found at `http://www.w3.org/TR/xpath`.

Additional Reading

- W3C. Extensible Markup Language (XML) 1.0, 2nd edition. W3C Recommendation, 6 October 2000. `http://www.w3.org/TR/2000/REC-cml-20001006.`
- W3C. XML in 10 points. `http://www.w3.org/XML/1999/XML-in-10-points.html`
- W3C. Extensible Markup Language (XML): Activity Statement. `http://www.w3.org/XMLActivity.html`
- W3C. Namespaces in XML. World Wide Web Consortium, 14 January 1999. `http://www.w3.org/TR/1999/REC-xml-names-19990114/`
- Simpson, John E.. *Just XML*. Location of publisher: Prentice-Hall Inc., 1999.
- Hjelm, Johan. *Designing Wireless Information Services*. New York: John Wiley & Sons, Inc., 2000.

Taking Charge of Profile Information Conveyance

Helena Lindskog, Ericsson
Prof. Simone Fischer-Hübner, Karlstad University
Mikael Nilsson, Ericsson

Introduction

The mobile Internet promises applications featuring rich content, comprising text, audio, and streaming video in full color. The range of possible services that can be developed using these features, together with the unique characteristics of mobile networks, is immense.

Mechanisms of the mobile Internet allow users to both access Internet services and other server-based applications from mobile devices and make new services possible, such as location-based and context-aware applications. Composite Capabilities/Preference Profile (CC/PP) is used to convey capability and preference information (CPI) when accessing Web resources to facilitate content adaptation to best fit the capabilities and preferences of the user-agents and users. While mobile services can be of great use, privacy risks need to be considered as well. With these new protocols or services, personal data such as location data, CPI, and further user attributes is transferred with messages and exposed at different nodes, such as the WAP gateway/proxy or the origin server's site. Appropriate legal and technical data protection and privacy safeguards must be implemented.

At Karlstad University, we have investigated privacy and privacy risks in the mobile Internet, as well as technical means for enhancing the user's privacy, in cooperation with Ericsson. Particularly, we have analyzed how the Platform for Privacy Preferences Project (P3P) protocol can be used to enforce the user's control over the release of CPI and location data (see also [Nilsson et al. 2001]). This appendix describes how PiMI enforces the user's right to self-determination.

Privacy

Privacy is well recognized as a fundamental human right. In general the concept of privacy has three aspects [Rosenberg 1992], [Holvast 1993]:

- **Privacy of the person**—by protecting a person against undue interference, such as physical searches or information violating his or her moral sense
- **Territorial privacy**—by protecting the close physical area surrounding a person
- **Informational privacy**—by controlling whether and how personal data can be gathered, stored, processed, or selectively disseminated

The first definition of privacy was given by the two American lawyers, Samuel D. Warren and Louis D. Brandeis, who in their famous article "The Right to Privacy," published in 1890, defined privacy as "the right to be let alone" [Warren & Brandeis 1890].

The most common definition of informational privacy in current use is the one by Alan Westin: "Privacy is the claim of individuals, groups, and institutions to determine for themselves, when, how, and to what extent information about them is communicated to others" [Westin 1967].

The emphasis of this appendix is on the discussion of informational privacy of individuals, which according to Westin's and other common definitions can be defined as the right of informational self-determination. Nevertheless, also in the mobile Internet, the problem of unsolicited commercial emails (spam) is increasingly affecting privacy in the sense of the right to be let alone. It can also be seen as an intrusion of territorial privacy and of privacy of the person (if indecent information is distributed). However, spamming will only be briefly addressed.

In order to protect the right of informational self-determination, data protection laws of mostly western states, as well as international privacy guidelines or directives (such as the EU Directive 95/46/EC on

Data Protection [EU Directive 1995]) and the OECD Privacy guidelines [OECD 1980], require basic privacy principles to be guaranteed when personal data is collected or processed. These include the following:

- *Legitimacy*: Personal data collection and processing is admissible only if permitted by legal provisions or if the data subject has consented (Art. 7).
- *Purpose specification and purpose binding*: Personal data must be obtained for specified and legitimate purposes and should not be used for other purposes (Art. 6).
- *Necessity of data collection and processing*: The collection and processing of personal data shall be allowed only if it is necessary for the tasks falling within the responsibility of the data processing agency (Art. 7).
- *The data subject's right to information, notification, objection, and the right to correction, erasure, or blocking of incorrect or illegally stored data*: (Art. 10–14).
- *Supervision and sanctions*: Control for compliance by an independent supervisory authority (see Art. 28). Criminal or other penalties should be envisaged in the event of noncompliance
- *Requirement of adequate technical and organizational security mechanisms to guarantee the confidentiality, integrity, and availability of personal data*: (Art. 6, 17).

Provisions of the EUDirective 95/46/EC on Data Protection as well as national data protection laws also apply to the collection and processing of personal data in the mobile Internet environment. Nevertheless, more specific privacy requirements for the mobile Internet environment were recently formulated in the Proposal for a Directive of the European Parliament and of the Council concerning the processing of personal data and the protection of privacy in the electronic communication sector (COM (2000) 385) [EU Directive-Proposal 2000]. This proposed new directive is intended to replace the directive 97/66/EC concerning the processing of personal data and the protection of privacy in the telecommunication sector [EU Telecommunication Directive 1997].

In addition to the protection of traffic data, the proposed directive COM (2000) 385 addresses also location data giving the geographic location of mobile users or, more precisely, of their devices. According to Art. 9 I, location data may be processed only when it is anonymous or with the consent of the users or subscribers to the extent and for the duration necessary for the provision of a value-added service. Also, according to Art. 9 II, where consent of users has been obtained, the user must continue to have the possibility of temporarily refusing the processing of location data for each connection to the network or for each transmission of the communication. Exceptions are formulated for emergency services (Art. 10) and for necessary measures to safeguard security, defense, and crime investigations (Art. 15).

In addition, Art. 13 introduces an opt-in system for unsolicited electronic mail and thus bans spam.

Mobile Internet Architecture and Services

WAP 1.2.1 Architecture

"The Wireless Application Protocol (WAP) is an open, global specification that empowers mobile users with wireless devices to easily access and interact with information and services instantly" [WAP]. The version used in current products is WAP 1.2.1. It describes how to send requests and responses over a wireless connection, using the Wireless Session Protocol (WSP), which is an extended and bytecoded version of HTTP 1.1 [WSP]. Typically, a WSP request is sent from a mobile device to a WAP Gateway/Proxy (WAP Gateway), from where an HTTP session with the target Web server is established [WBXML]. Over this session, the WSP request, converted into HTTP, is sent. The content, typically presented in the Wireless Mark-up Language (WML), is sent back to the WAP Gateway, where it is bytecoded and sent to the device over the WSP session.

WAP 2.0

The next version of WAP, which is to be released in the first quarter of 2002, relies on similar components as in WAP 1.2.1. The main difference is that the user equipment (UE) communicates with the origin server via a feature enhancing proxy directly over HTTP, as shown in Figure B.1. The protocol stack in the mobile device is a Wireless Profiled (WP) TCP/IP stack. An important difference is that the use of a proxy/gateway now is optional, which means that the UE can issue HTTP requests over TCP/IP directly to the origin server, with no intermediaries.

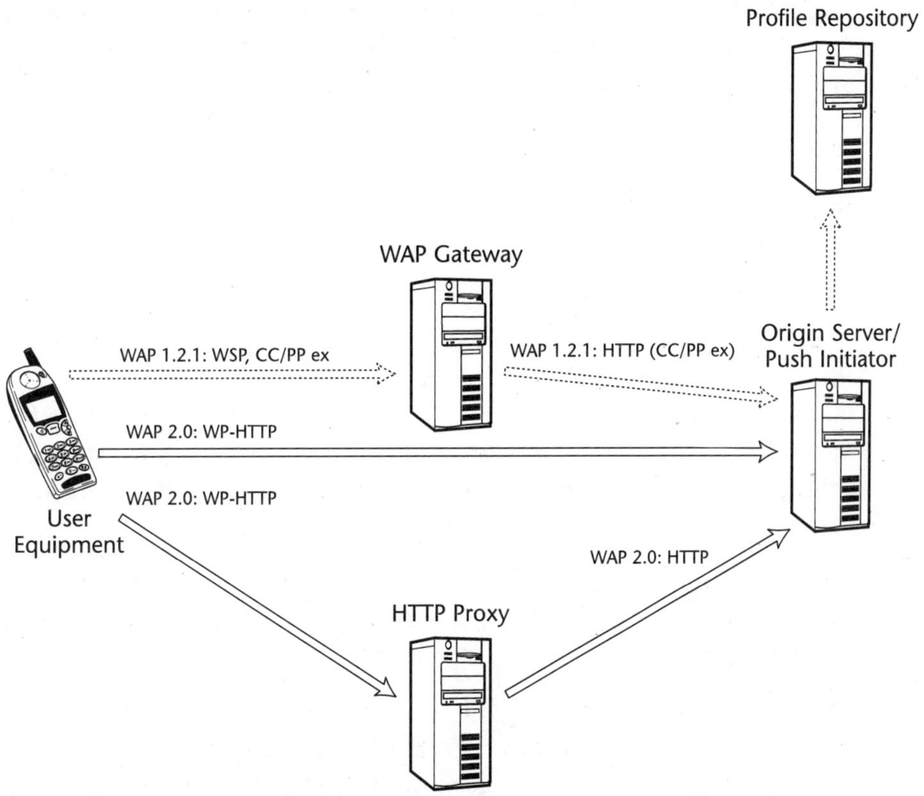

Figure B.1 WAP 1.2.1 and WAP 2.0 programming models.

On the application layer, the use of WML-specific extensions has been made optional. The WAP Forum standard XHTML Mobile Profile—a derivative of XHTML—replaces WML as the markup language. This means that mobile devices now can access a large portion of legacy, non–XML-based HTML Web sites directly, with no need for content translation or transcoding.

Personal Trusted Devices

The vision of the largest mobile device manufacturers, Ericsson, Nokia, and Motorola, and other companies in the industry [MeT Overview 2001] is to broaden the role of the mobile phone. The device might be used for identification, authorization, payment, and ticket storage and validation. This implies storage of private keys, certificates, credit card numbers, and identity units, typically stored in the subscriber identity module (SIM) card. Mechanisms for signing and a Bluetooth connection or similar are also needed. The MeT initiative implements these ideas [MeT Overview 2001].

User-Agent Profiles

Composite Capabilities/Preferences Profile (CC/PP) by the World Wide Web Consortium (W3C) specifies how a client-side user-agent, such as a Web browser in a PC or a mobile phone, can deliver a description of its capabilities and the users' settings to an origin server. This is done so that an application on the origin server can generate content tailored to the characteristics and Man-Machine Interface (MMI) of the requesting device, thus enhancing the user experience and minimizing the use of bandwidth.

CC/PP is defined as an application of the meta-data framework Resource Description Framework (RDF), which is, in turn, an XML application.

What is required by CC/PP is that the description is done using a vocabulary. This results in a Capabilities and Preference Information (CPI) profile. This XML document comprises a set of components, within which attributes describing the user-agent and device reside. It is expected that users of CC/PP define a vocabulary pertinent to their specific application.

CC/PP ex is a protocol defined for transmitting CPI over HTTP. It uses the HTTP extension framework, which is a mechanism that allows you to define new protocols on top of HTTP.

The User-Agent Profile (UAProf) Drafting Committee of the WAP Forum created a specification [UAProf 2001] based on the original CC/PP note [CC/PP Note 1999] including some WAP specific extensions.

The information sent with CC/PP can be divided into three categories:

- Device information (which device you are using and its capabilities) and network characteristics
- User settings (some preferences of the user)
- User information (prestored user information or other context-dependent information, such as location)

Location-Based Services

Passing on the user's geographical location to the service provider opens up a whole range of new possible features [Hjelm et al. 2000], many on the theme "find the nearest . . . ." Most developers of WAP-related software today provide such a feature for telecom operators. With Global Positioning System (GPS) devices or such, it is not likely that operators will be the only service providers that will receive this kind of information.

The methods for location passing vary. The following are possible:

- The device knows its own location, using GPS or some related technology, and passes it on with the request—for example, by using a proprietary HTTP header or the attributes available in UAProf, which can be used by the mobile device for conveying location information to origin servers.
- The operator of a PLMN/GSM network knows the user's location through base station information and makes calculations from the strength of the signal within different cells.

Context-Aware Services

A context-aware service is an Internet service knowledgeable about the environment in which it and its user operate. Schilit [1995] has defined context-aware services: "Application adaptation triggered by such things as the location of use, the collection of nearby people, the presence of accessible devices and other kinds of objects, as well as changes to all these things over time."

The concept of context awareness includes a lot of parameters, which can be divided into the major types: activity, identity, location, and time.

The data required to implement context-aware services can be collected in several different ways in a mobile network. Parlay [3GPP] provides a CORBA interface to SS7, SMS [ETSI GSM 03.71] provides a text-based interface to SS7 and location information as data can be sent to/from clients in a generic way. Finally, standard/nonstandard HTTP headers can be used to submit information to an application server.

Privacy Risks

Risks Factors

Privacy in mobile Internet environments is a much greater issue than privacy in traditional Internet environments, due to the following four issues:

1. **The small screens.** The fact that devices have smaller screens means that personalization is a much bigger issue in the mobile Internet than in traditional Internet environments, where personalization of sites is a matter of convenience to the end user. Personalization implies behavior tracking and profiling through log files, user databases or cookies, and user settings. In a mobile Internet environment, surfing will hardly be worthwhile if you cannot retrieve the information that you wish in a few clicks.
2. **The wireless connection to the Internet.** There are mainly two kinds of wireless connections:
   - **Digital cellular systems—for example, GSM.** When using a digital cellular system, the telecom operator already knows your whereabouts. The mobile Internet does not today bring the possibility of tracking end users through IP numbers and traceroute commands, but there is a possibility that we will see such scenarios in the future.
   - **Short-range radio links—for example, Bluetooth.** When using short-range radio links, the user is exposed to a new group of service providers, which are not as well acquainted with handling personal information (for example, shop owners or public transportation providers).

In this case, there is also a new kind of territorial privacy threats; see the Privacy section. In other words, a Bluetooth mobile Internet service provider, such as a train company or a retailer, can collect information about the end user, when the end user is close to the provider's Bluetooth access points, and then reuse this information to send personalized, and possibly unwanted, messages to the end user.

3. **The portability.** The chance to carry the device with you everywhere you go gives you a whole new range of possible services. Many of those require your position, in X and Y coordinates, but

some might trigger other things, such as the room that you just entered (see Context-Aware Services) or the fact that you are physically close to another person. A personal trusted device (see Personal Trusted Devices) will provide you with the possibility to use your device instead of identity cards, credit cards, or bonus cards.

4. **The difference in device capabilities.** When requesting a URL within a traditional Internet environment, the device information that is normally transmitted over HTTP 1.1 [RFC 2616] is only the user-agent. Because most people use Internet Explorer or Netscape browsers, this information tells little about the user. With user-agent profiles of small devices, much more information about the end user will be transmitted; see [UAProf 2001].

Exposed Data

As discussed in [Nilsson et al. 2001], a side-effect of mobile Internet communication is that traffic data, location data, user preferences, and user or device characteristics that are transferred with a message as well as content data are exposed at different nodes and can be used to create communication profiles.

The request will pass through a number of components inside the operator's environment. The operator holds information about the user's location and traffic data needed for transmission of a request. In contrast to origin servers and WAP gateways that could be placed in non-trustworthy domains, operators are usually better able to handle private information, due to the fact that they normally risk heavy penalties otherwise. Furthermore, most Western countries have legal provisions—for instance, for processing and storing traffic data.

In WAP 1.x systems, the WAP gateway is the aggregation point of all requests. Because the WAP gateway unpacks all the layers in the stack, the requests, parameters, and content, together with capability and preference information (CPI), location data, and other user identifying data (Bluetooth ID, MSISDN), can easily be seen here. As the user usually uses just one or a small number of WAP gateways, such personal information related with all requests of a user can be aggregated at the WAP gateway. Although WAP gateways are often used as anonymizers to filter out personal data such as the MSISDN number. Their profiling capability makes them, together with the origin servers, the critical components from a privacy perspective.

Personal user data can also be accumulated at the origin server's site. Besides the requests, parameters, CPI, location data, and other user identifying data that are forwarded by the WAP gateway to the origin server or requested by the origin server (in the case of Web page logon), the origin server site can also post cookies and store session data (time, type of transaction) and data about transferred files. Origin servers might be placed in countries without or with no stringent privacy legislation, and it is often unclear how far they can be trusted to respect the user's privacy.

As pointed out in [Nilsson et al. 2001], all exposed personal data can be sensitive dependent on the context and the purpose of its use. It is quite obvious that collecting location data and thus tracing the user's location is a severe privacy threat. However, information about the device capabilities and the user's preferences can become very sensitive if used in a certain context. For instance, the user's voice and graphic settings can reveal information about a user's visual or auditory (dis)abilities. Also, that a user owns an expensive mobile phone could be misused by malicious attackers.

Spam

The low prices of bulk email and pseudonyms are contributing factors to the spam problem [Cranor & LaMacchia 1998]. Now this problem has appeared in the mobile Internet as well. Large amounts of unwanted junk mail make it difficult or time-consuming for the recipients to access their wanted mails, and users also have to pay for downloading them. Another privacy issue is that pornographic advertisements in junk mails may violate the recipient's moral sense.

Though this appendix mainly treats informational privacy, the spam problem is one of the most common results of improper handling of personal data. On top of email messages and SMS messages, pushed Web sites, such as WAP Push and Bluetooth advertisements, may harm the end user.

Spamming of all kinds must be addressed by both regulatory and technical means. An opt-in system for unsolicited mails, as proposed by the draft EU Directive COM (2000) 385, will surely help to reduce spamming. Nevertheless, as identifying and suing all junk mail senders might not be practical, further technical means, such as filtering systems, need to be enforced by the service provider.

Privacy-Enhancing Technologies

Basic Concepts

There are two major ways to enhance privacy in the mobile Internet with technology. Privacy can be protected most effectively by technologies that avoid or at least minimize the personal data exposed at network sites and thus provide anonymity, pseudonymity, unlinkability, or unobservability. Such technologies cannot be applied in applications where personal data has to be processed.

Other privacy technologies can technically control that personal data is used only according to legal provisions. P3P is a technology that enforces that personal data is forwarded only with the user's informed consent. According to data protection legislation, informed user consent is often required for the legitimacy of data processing.

Platform for Privacy Preference Project (P3P)

Self-determination for end users is a key issue. People's views of privacy differ a lot between individuals, and our willingness to give away information in exchange for convenience must be respected.

One simple way to accomplish this would be to ask the end user before making a transaction. To increase usability, we need to find a way for the user to enter personal settings once and for all, without having to reenter them for each connection.

P3P provides developers of user agents, such as Web and WAP browsers, with a specific privacy policy format that can be parsed and matched against the end user's preferences.

P3P Agreement

How a P3P agreement is done is fully described in [P3P]. The P3P user-agent will typically, when an HTTP request is made, fetch a reference file, which is a site map, matching the policy file with pages or parts of the site, and which is typically stored at a well-known location at a Web site, "/w3c/p3p.xml". According to this reference file, the appropriate policy file will be retrieved and matched against the user's preferences. If there is a match, the page will be requested, and if not, the user-agent will take some kind of action to warn the user.

During the agreement, little or no information needs to be submitted. Minimal data collection should take place, and data that is collected is used in only nonidentifiable form. This is called the "safe-zone."

A P3P User Agent

There will be various kinds of P3P user agents:

- Plug-ins, browser built-ins, or proxies
- Those that only inform the user and those that will take some kind of action
- Those that perform agreement on the user's explicit demand or always

In mobile devices, user agents will be built in, apparently, but proxies that act as trusted third parties are also possible. When we say trusted, we mean that in order to be responsible for the tremendous amounts of personal data that such a proxy would hold, trust is absolutely necessary.

The PiMI Prototype

We suggest that CC/PP be used together with P3P to ensure the end user's right to self-determination. As discussed in Privacy Risks, this is particularly important in mobile Internet environments.

The PiMI Prototype project started as a joint venture between Ericsson and Karlstad University in March 2001. The PiMI project goal was to implement P3P user agents controlling the dissemination of CPI in mobile Internet environments by the means of Minimal Profile Conveyance (see the next section) as described in [Nilsson et al. 2001].

Minimal Profile Conveyance

CPI is represented by means of a profile (see User-Agent Profiles), which comprises a set of components. Each component is a placeholder for related attributes.

In [Nilsson et al. 2001], we suggest that the user define a minimal CPI profile, containing only information that he or she considers completely harmless or where there is an understanding that this information may be necessary for some reason. This minimal profile can be used for the following purposes:

- To access non–P3P-enabled Web sites or Web sites that do not meet the user's P3P privacy preferences
- To serve third-party requests to the WAP gateway for cached profiles (such as for WAP push content generation)
- To communicate in the safe-zone before a P3P agreement (within the "safe-zone," however, no CPI is needed, so that a completely empty profile could be used instead)

The end user also has to define a full CPI profile to be used when there is a successful P3P agreement on a general basis—that is, the site is P3P compatible, and the general information in the site's P3P policy file suits the end user's privacy preferences. All CPI attributes in this full profile must be agreed upon; there must be a P3P policy statement that corresponds to the end user's preferences for these attributes. Otherwise, the CPI attributes will not be transmitted.

The WSP suspend and resume mechanisms can be used for retransmission of the data in the full profile that has been agreed upon.

Overview

The PiMI system consists of both a proxy-based and a browser built-in P3P user-agent (see Figure B.2). The browser built-in user-agent solution guarantees that the user has direct control over his or her privacy preferences. The communication during the P3P agreement over WSP [WSP], though, is quite slow and costly. With the proxy-based solution, the user-agent's communication during a P3P agreement is done by an HTTP privacy proxy and thus takes place via wireline communication. As in this case, the proxy has control over the user's privacy preferences; it should be under direct control of either a trusted third party (TTP) or the user (for example, runnning on the user's PC).

In the prototype project, we have so far developed only P3P preferences and policies for CPI information. A sample P3P policy file for UAProf attributes, written for the project, can be found at [P3P & UAProf]. The concept can also be used for any other kind of personal data to be transmitted from the device: location data, name, credit card number, and so on.

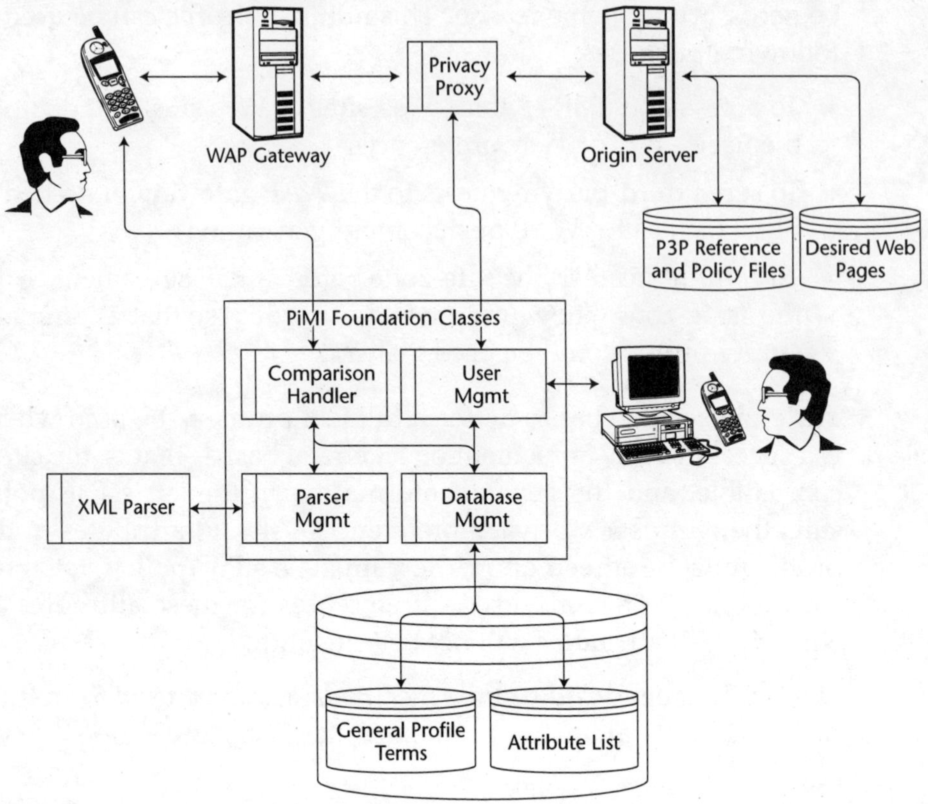

Figure B.2 PiMI architecture.

In this prototype, we test only for CPI information. The same principle, however, can be used for any other kind of data to be transmitted from the device: location data, name, credit card number, and so on.

Both the browser built-in and proxy user-agents use the PiMI foundation classes that allow the end user to enter preferences from an HTML as well as a WML interface and have them stored in flat files.

The comparison handler will retrieve the reference file according to the well-known location concept, find the policy file—for example, the one described in [P3P & UAProf]—and compare the general information (in this case, access information). If there is a match, it will compare the data in the full profile; otherwise, it will compare the data in the minimal profile. After this, it will either retrieve the Web page, passing on the information agreed upon, or warn the end user about the parts that failed and ask whether he or she consents to providing the information.

Results and Suggestions

The number of attributes for which a P3P agreement has to be made widely exceeds the number of attributes used in traditional Web environments, as discussed in Privacy Risks.

We realize that it is wise to use three categories for each CPI attribute:

Minimal. This attribute is part of the minimal profile and can be given away to any site.

Full. This attribute is part of the full profile and can be given if the user's preferences for this attribute match the site's policy (that is, the user gives his or her implicit consent).

Never. This attribute will never be given away without the end user's explicit consent (that is, the user is explicitly asked).

It is technically possible to have the end user define a range of profiles and select among them before each transmission. There is a conflict between user friendliness and privacy friendliness. The principle tried in the PiMI project is one first step toward self-determination without disturbing the end user more than necessary.

Use Case

In this use case, we have an end user, Alice, who is willing to give away image capability—the fact that she can view images and screen size (the size of the screen in pixels)—in order to get a better experience when viewing a page. To some sites that she visits often, and to sites that will grant her access to all the information that they store, she may be willing to give away the browser name as well. That is, she may reveal the name of the user-agent, so that everything about the browser and its capabilities can be fetched by the origin server, the exact browser version. She never wants sites to know her name without asking first, even though it is stored in the device.

In the device, Alice has the following options:

1. "I consider the following sites to be 'reliable'":
2. "I also consider sites reliable under the following circumstances":

CONDITION	THIS MAKES THE SITE...
Web site does not collect identified data.	Reliable/Not reliable
Access is given to all identified data.	Reliable/Not reliable
Access is given to identified online and physical contact information as well as to certain other identified data.	Reliable/Not reliable
Access is given to identified online and physical contact information (for example, users can access things such as a postal address).	Reliable/Not reliable
Access is given to certain other identified data (for example, users can access things such as their online account charges).	Reliable/Not reliable
No access to identified data is given.	Reliable/Not reliable

"This is how I view my personal data":

INFORMATION	THIS CAN BE SENT...
I want color images	Always/To reliable sites/Never
My pixel size	Always/To reliable sites/Never
The name of my browser	Always/To reliable sites/Never
The version of my browser	Always/To reliable sites/Never
My name	Always/To reliable sites/Never

The choices can be more granular—for example, "The version of my browser can be sent always, assuming it is not retained, to reliable sites assuming the recipient is only ourselves." Making the conditions user friendly is a challenge for usability experts, and the topic will not be treated here.

When the agreement takes place, the first step is to decide whether the site is to be considered reliable. The next step is to match the data that is required in the policy (see [P3P & UAProf]), and finally the policy is matched with the preferences of the end user; if the match goes through, Alice's data is sent. If not, Alice is asked whether she wants to submit the data anyway. This way, Alice is disturbed as little as possible, and her user-agent does what user-agents are for: It handles her data according to her wishes until there is a mismatch.

Enhancement of P3P's Operation Environment

P3P can enhance the user's privacy by informing him or her about a Web site's privacy practices and letting the user decide independently of that privacy policy what personal data for what purposes he or she wants to reveal. Nevertheless, P3P has several weaknesses and limitations (see also [EPIC 2000]).

First of all, P3P does not provide a technical mechanism for making sure that sites ask only for necessary personal information and that sites act according to their policies. Hence, whereas P3P can implement informed consent, it does not support other essential provisions of the EU-Directive, such as Art. 6b (purpose binding), Art. 6c, Art. 7 (necessity of data collection and processing), and Art. 12 (right of access). Thus, P3P alone is not a sufficient solution. Privacy advocates have actually even expressed their concerns that P3P can in practice be used to push users to give up their privacy by forcing them to reveal more personal data than necessary in exchange for the provision of a service.

According to German Multimedia Legislation (§3 (3) Teleservices Data Protection Act - TDDSG), the service provider may not make the use of services conditional on the consent of the user to the effect that this data may be processed or used for other purposes than necessary, if other access to these services is not reasonably provided to the users. Corresponding regulations should be established at the international level.

A further step within our research project will be to work on a proposal for how P3P can be augmented with other security mechanisms to support the implementation of basic privacy requirements of the EU data protection directive at the Web server's site: In a former research project, a formal privacy model was developed and implemented in the Linux system kernel [Fischer-Hübner et al. 1998], [Fischer-Hübner 2001]. The privacy model has been designed as an access control model that can technically enforce legal privacy requirements such as purpose restriction and necessity of data processing. It is planned to adapt the privacy model implementation so that it can be used in combination with third-party monitoring and assurance to protect P3P data elements at the server's site in order to ensure that personal data elements are collected and processed only as necessary and are used only for the specified purposes.

Conclusion

In this appendix, we have discussed why the user's privacy is at risk in the mobile Internet. To protect privacy, a holistic approach, including legal means, privacy-enhancing technologies, and educational measures for raising awareness and teaching users how to apply privacy-enhancing technologies, is needed.

Legal privacy requirements for the mobile Internet environment were recently formulated in the Proposal for an EU Directive concerning the processing of personal data and the protection of privacy in the electronic communication sector [EU Directive-Proposal 2000]. The proposed directive addresses the protection of location data and requires that location data may be processed only when it is made anonymous or with the consent of the users or subscribers to the extent and for the duration necessary for the provision of a value added service.

The P3P protocol can be used to enforce user control over personal user data, such as CPI including location data, allowing the transfer of CPI and location data only if there is an informed consent of the user. Thus, the WAP P3P user agents developed in the PiMI prototype project can be used to protect location data according to the requirement of the EU directive proposal.

References

[3GPP] "3G Partnership Project." http://www.3gpp.org/.

[CC/PP Note 1999] F. Reynolds, J. Hjelm, S. Dawkins, and S. Singhal. "CC/PP: A user side framework for content negotiation." *W3C Note*. July 1999. http://www.w3.org/TR/NOTE-CCPP/.

[CC/PP] World Wide Web Consortium. "Composite Capability/Preference Profiles (CC/PP): Structure and Vocabularies." *W3C Working Draft*. 15 March 2001. http://www.w3.org/TR/CCPP-struct-vocab/.

[Cranor & LaMacchia 1998] L. Cranor and B. LaMacchia. "Spam!" *Communications of the ACM*. Vol. 41, No. 8. August 1998. http://lorrie.cranor.org/pubs/spam/spam.html.

[EPIC 2000] Electronic Privacy Information Center (EPIC). "Pretty Poor Privacy: An Assessment of P3P and Internet Privacy." June 2000. http://www.epic.org/reports/prettypoorprivacy.html.

[ETSI GSM 03.71] ETSI Specification GSM 03.71 V7.3.0. "ETSI Technical Specification GSM 03.71." February 2000.

[EU Directive 1995] Directive 95/46/EC of the European Parliament and of the Council of 24 October 1995 on the protection of individuals with regard to the processing of personal data and on the free movement of such data. http://europa.eu.int/ISPO/legal/en/dataprot/directiv/directiv.html.

[EU Directive-Proposal 2000] Commission of the European Communities COM(2000) 385. "Proposal for a Directive of the European Parliament and of the Council." July 2000. http://europa.eu.int/comm/information_society/policy/framework/pdf/com2000385_en.pdf.

[EU Telecommunication Directive 1997] European Parliament. "Directive 97/66/EC of the European Parliament and of the Council Concerning the Processing of Personal Data and the Protection of Privacy in the Telecommunications Sector of 15 December 1997."

[Fischer-Hübner 2001] S. Fischer-Hübner. "IT-Security and Privacy—Design and Use of Privacy-Enhancing Security Mechansims." *Springer Scientific Publishers, Lecture Notes of Computer Science, LNCS 1958.* May 2001.

[Fischer-Hübner et al. 1998] S. Fischer-Hübner, A. Ott,. "From a Formal Privacy Model to its Implementation." *Proceedings of the 21st National Information Systems Security Conference.* Arlington, VA. October 5-8, 1998.

[Hjelm et al. 2000] J. Hjelm and M. Nilsson. "Position dependent services using metadata profile matching." *iNet, the Internet Society Conference.* July 2000. http://www.wireless-information.net/Johan/Engelska/inet00-paper-01.htm.

[Holvast 1993] J. Holvast. "Vulnerability and Privacy: Are We on the Way to a Risk-Free Society?" *J.Berleur et al. (Ed.): Facing the Challenge of Risk and Vulnerability in an Information Society, Proceedings of the IFIP-WG9.2 Conference.* Elsevier Science Publishers B.V. (North-Holland), 1993. Namur May 20-22, 1993.

[MeT Overview 2001] "MeT Overview White Paper, Version 2.0." January 29, 2001. http://www.mobiletransaction.org/pdf/White%20Paper_2.0.pdf.

[Nilsson et al. 2001] M. Nilsson, H. Lindskog, and S. Fischer-Hübner. "Privacy Enhancement in the Mobile Internet." In *Proceedings of Security and Control of IT in Society-II, IFIP SCITS-II*. Bratislava, Slovakia, June 15-16, 2001. http://privacy.lindskog.ws/pimi.pdf.

[OECD 1980] Organisation for Economic Cooperation and Development. "Recommendation of the Council Concerning Guidelines Governing the Protection of Privacy and Transborder Flows of Personal Data." 23 September 1980.

[P3P & UAProf] H. Lindskog. "A Sample P3P Policy for UAProf." May 2001. http://privacy.lindskog.ws/p3p_policy4uaprof.html.

[P3P] World Wide Web Consortium. "The Platform for Privacy Preferences 1.0 (P3P1.0) Specification." *W3C Working Draft*. 28 September 2001. http://www.w3.org/TR/P3P/.

[RFC 2616] R. Fielding et al. "Hypertext Transfer Protocol—HTTP/1.1." *World Wide Web Consortium*. June 1999. http://www.w3.org/Protocols/rfc2068/rfc2068.

[Rosenberg 1992] R. Rosenberg. "The Social Impact of Computers." *Academic Press*. 1992.

[Schilit 1995] W. Schilit. "A System Architecture for Context-Aware Mobile Computing." 1995. http://www.fxpal.xerox.com/people/schilit/index.htm.

[UAProf 2001] WAP Forum. "User Agent Profile Specification." *WAP Forum Working Draft*. 2001. http://www.wapforum.org/.

[WAP] WAP Forum. "Wireless Application Protocol, Wireless Application Protocol Specification." 2001. http://www.wapforum.org/.

[WBXML] WAP Forum. "Wireless Application Protocol, WAP Binary XML." *WAP-192-WBXML*. 25 -July 2000. http://www.wapforum.org/.

[WSP] WAP Forum. "Wireless Application Protocol, Wireless Session Protocol Specification." *WAP-203-WSP*. 4 -May 2000. http://www.wapforum.org/.

[Warren & Brandeis 1890] S. D. Warren and L. D. Brandeis. "The Right to Privacy." *Harvard Law Review*. 15 December 1890.

[Westin 1967] A. Westin. "Privacy and Freedom." New York, 1967.

A P3P Use Case

Telia is the largest Swedish telecom operator. Telia Internet Services is responsible for the Group's Internet services: accesses and applications. The business area offers Internet services to consumers and business customers in Sweden and other Nordic countries. Comhem.se is the start page to Telia's broadband connection in Sweden and Denmark. At its Web site, it is possible to download content, such as streaming video and games. Video on demand will be realized in the near future. We are using Telia's privacy policy as an example in this appendix.

The Driving Force behind the P3P Implementation

It was in July 2002 that Magnus Johnard and I decided to work on Telia's policies together. Very few sites in Sweden are fully P3P enabled, and this is a big site with 330,000 unique visitors per day, so it would serve as a good example for most Web site owners. The initiating reason for implementing P3P was, as for most Web site owners, that the company's customers got Internet Explorer 6 and started to complain about the third-party cookies, either that some considered them to be spyware and did not want them (we do not agree with this, though) or that the advertisement was not rotating anymore because Internet Explorer 6 blocked the third-party cookies that keep track of how many times a customer has seen an ad. Sometimes customers had problems logging in to the system because the session cookie was blocked by IE 6.0; therefore the system did not recognize the customer as logged in.

There are two sides to third-party cookies, of course. To some people it is a blessing not having to see the same ad all the time; others get terribly upset by the mere idea of having their data transmitted to external sites. The need for privacy is a personal matter, as we have discussed earlier in this book.

The blocking of third-party cookies is not normally a problem for a Web site owner, but it is a problem for the third-party cookie provider. At this site, advertising was being placed by Telia's Danish domain, which has the top domain .dk for Denmark instead of .se for Sweden (see Figure C.1).

Cookie filtering is a technical solution to an ethical and legal problem. What may be considered a first-party cookie legally and ethically—the Danish domain belongs to the same company—may sometimes be a third-party cookie technically, which was what happened in this case.

Regardless of the problems of the customers—too much privacy or lack of privacy—a P3P policy would help solve both. Sweden falls under European privacy legislation, and the site collects only what it is allowed to according to law, so there is no legal driving force to implement P3P. Providing a policy that might help users find privacy information or allow future P3P user-agents to make the right decisions based on the privacy of the Web site would be a great benefit to the company's end users.

What Happened?

First, we met to discuss what needed to be done. Magnus read a draft of the manuscript of this book, to get a better understanding of the implications of P3P.

The next step was to collect information about data collected from the customers and to craft this information into a human-readable privacy policy. This work involved having discussions with both the implementers and the company lawyer. You can find this policy at the end of this appendix. Magnus also decided to create an opt-in and opt-out page, with information about the choices that the end user has. The third step was to create the P3P in XML reference and policy files. This took a couple of hours altogether. The fourth step was to store all the files at the designated location and to test them through validators and Internet Explorer and Netscape viewers.

About the Web Site

The Web site is divided into two parts. One is public, open to everybody, and the other is private, open only to customers who have accounts. There are also two types of accounts: one for everybody and one for those who have signed a financial agreement, allowing the company to charge them for what they buy, especially content download. In order to get such an account, a financial clearance is made, and a letter is sent home to the customer.

Figure C.1 The Telia Comhem.se Web site.

Because the restricted area—that is, the area where the customers have to logon to get access—is at another domain, we needed to have two reference files, one for each domain. There is one policy file for the open area and one for the restricted area. We would have had that even if the areas had been at the same domain because the practices are very different.

At both areas they use security log files. Their practices for security are not be revealed in this book because security practices should be kept secret from intruders, and they are stored no longer than necessary to be able to trace intruders.

No other data is stored or processed in the open area. First-party cookies are not set. Advertisers sometimes set third-party cookies. There is a disclaiming clause in the human-readable policy about this.

We now go through the different files that are stored and their respective locations.

The Human-Readable Policy

The human-readable policy, originally in Swedish but here translated to English, is stored at the location www.comhem.se/privacy/policy.html. Please note that the location may have changed since this book was printed.

Please note that this policy not only contains information about the practices of the Web site but also instructs the reader about privacy in general and about related information.

Telia Internet Services Privacy Policy

Valid from October 2002.

Confidentiality and cautiousness when handling personal data are of great importance to Telia because the relation to and confidence from our customers and Web site visitors are vital to our business. Telia always prioritizes privacy.

This Privacy Policy concerns Web pages whose URLs are located at the main domains:

- comhem.se

- http(s)://zone.tewss.telia.se/

"Telia" and "we" should be understood as Telia Internet Services AB, which is part of the Telia Corporation, and the other Telia companies that are represented at the URLs mentioned previously.

CONTENT

Below you can find Telia's Privacy Policy for:

- Personal information that is provided at our Web sites
- The use of cookies
- The use of security log files

CONTACT INFORMATION

If you have questions or comments regarding our privacy policy or its application, please contact:

Telia Internet Services
Box 7817
103 96 Stockholm
Sweden
Email: telia-comhem- redaktionen@telia.se

ABOUT THIS POLICY

Telia reserves the right to change this privacy policy when applicable legislation or the general development of the Internet requires this. Changes may take place at any time and will be announced on this Web page. We will specifically inform you who are our customers about major changes.

When creating this privacy policy, Telia has considered the European Privacy Directive (2000) 385, which was accepted by the European Parliament in May 2002. However, the directive will not be implemented until 2003. Among other issues, it contains rules regarding email and SMS marketing, where consent by the receiver is required.

Companies that obtained personal data directly from their customers are always entitled to market their products. Another change from the previous directive 95/46/EC is that clear and comprehensive information about the use of cookies must be found at a Web site.

As an Internet Service Provider we are well aware of how the Internet has changed and simplified your everyday life. The advantages that the Internet brings are at stake if customers and visitors do not feel that their right to privacy is properly respected. Telia is therefore striving to provide you with Internet services in such a way that your right to privacy is respected.

Telia assures you that:

- We will not use personal data without your explicit consent, except when necessary to provide you with services that you explicitly asked for

(continues)

- You will be able to control the data that you voluntarily provided us
- You have the opportunity to contact us with questions and comments on our way of handling your privacy

Telia is continuously working with improvement for the functions that are needed to handle the data that you provided us. Therefore, please visit this site regularly to be updated about the improvements made.

Storage and use of personal data

WHAT IS PERSONAL DATA?

Personal data is information that relates to an individual, such as name, date of birth, email address, and such.

WHAT IS PERSONAL IDENTIFIABLE DATA?

By personal identifiable data we mean data that is not directly tied to an individual, such as data that provides information about how you use Telia's Web pages. Examples of such data are domain names and IP numbers that your computer uses, date and time of visits, access time, Web browser name and version, and other similar data.

This information will help us keep track of the habits of the visitors, such as average time of visit at different Web pages. We sometimes use this information to improve the Web site.

TELIA'S USE OF PERSONAL DATA

You can visit our site and use many of our services without needing to provide us with any personal data. It is only when you register as a customer or member that you are asked to give away personal data.

Most of our services do not require any registration; however, some require that you register in order to be able to use billing for a purchase. When registering, you are required to fill in certain fields (some mandatory and some optional) and to choose a username and password. For example, we need data to get in contact with you, like your first name and surname, email address, and regular address. The data is needed in a number of ways:

- To inform you about new functions and services (if you agreed to this)
- To show banners and information from the fields of interest that you provided us
- To show first and surname on the messages that are sent from your email account

The data can be sent to specifically selected partners if you agreed to this.

PERSONAL IDENTIFIABLE INFORMATION

Telia receives personal identifiable information even when visitors use our Web pages but are not our registered customers or members. We use this information to personalize our Web pages, to show advertisements or information that corresponds to your interest, or to improve our services in a general way.

DISCLOSURE OF PERSONAL DATA

Sometimes Telia is questioned about which members or customers we have. We never reveal the identity of our customers unless we are forced to do so by law. If an authority has legal rights to receive such information, the request will be granted.

USE OF COOKIES AND IP NUMBERS

WHAT IS A COOKIE, AND HOW IS IT USED?

We sometimes use so-called cookies at our Web site in order to personalize the Web pages. A cookie is a text string that your Web browser will store at the computer that you use or in your company profile. Cookies cannot start programs, and they do not contain viruses. The text is sent to our site at your next visit. Cookies cannot be read by sites other than the ones that sent them. Nor can they be read on demand, but only when you choose to visit our site again.

The purpose of cookies is to provide the user with a better experience through personalization of the Web site, which can be done because the user is recognized throughout the visits. For example, we can rotate advertisements and make sure that you get quick access to the content you prefer.

You can decide whether you wish to accept cookies. Most Web browsers, such as Internet Explorer and Netscape, will accept cookies automatically, but you can manually change this through the options. If you turn off cookies, you will not be able to take full advantage of the Web and of our services.

THE USE OF IP NUMBERS

IP numbers are unique numbers that are automatically provisioned to the computer when you start using the Internet or a local network. Our Web site can sometimes identify your computer through your IP number. Some companies and networks use dynamic addresses, which means that the IP number will change from time to time. Thus, an IP number is sometimes an identifier, sometimes not. They can usually indicate which network you are using—for example, which company you work for.

Telia registers IP numbers for several purposes. The main reason is security. If there is an intrusion, or an attempt, we must be able to track the intruder. Another purpose is to be able to provide our advertisers with anonymous information about the visits to our Web sites. We never tie the IP number to a specific person unless there is a security attack.

THIRD-PARTY RELATIONS

We clearly state the names of companies that we work with at our Web site. The privacy practices of these Web sites are not included in this policy. Therefore, you should carefully study the privacy policies of these companies, and from these determine whether you want to continue to use their services.

(continues)

SECURITY

Telia has secure networks that are protected with firewalls. Passwords are used for user authentication. We have a number of security features to protect you against loss, misuse, and alteration of the personal data that you have provided us.

Very few of our personnel have access to your personal data. Telia has very strict rules that apply to employees with access to the user databases and the servers that provide our services. Telia cannot guarantee that loss, misuse, or data alteration will not occur; however, we work actively to ensure that this does not happen.

Besides this file, another file containing information about where to opt in and opt out was created and stored under the name preferences.html, in the w3c directory. It contains links to pages where choices can be made and where personal data is provided or removed.

The P3P Files of the Comhem Domain

The reference file of the Comhem domain, where everybody has access, is very short because there is only one policy that is valid for the entire domain.

www.comhem.se/w3c/p3p.xml

Here you can see that the policy file is stored in the w3c folder, just like the reference file.

```
<META xmlns="http://www.w3.org/2002/01/P3Pv1">
 <POLICY-REFERENCES>
  <EXPIRY max-age="86400"/>

    <POLICY-REF about="/w3c/policy.xml">
      <INCLUDE>/*</INCLUDE>
    </POLICY-REF>
 </POLICY-REFERENCES>
</META>
```

www.comhem.se/w3c/policy.xml

The policy file of the open domain is very short. No cookies are used, and the only user data collected is security log files.

```
<POLICIES xmlns="http://www.w3.org/2002/01/P3Pv1">
 <POLICY name="default"
     discuri="http://www.comhem.se/privacy/policy.html"
     opturi=" http://www.comhem.se/privacy/preferences.html"
     xml:lang="en">
  <ENTITY>
   <DATA-GROUP>
    <DATA ref="#business.name">Telia Internet Services</DATA>
    <DATA ref="#business.contact-info.postal.street">Box 7817</DATA><
    <DATA ref="#business.contact-info.postal.postalcode">103 96</DATA>
    <DATA ref="#business.contact-info.postal.city">Stockholm</DATA>
    <DATA ref="#business.contact-info.postal.country">Sweden</DATA>
    <DATA ref="#business.contact-info.online.email">telia-comhem-redak-
tionen@telia.se</DATA>
    <DATA ref="#business.contact-
info.telecom.telephone.intcode">46</DATA>
    <DATA ref="#business.contact-
info.telecom.telephone.loccode">20</DATA>
    <DATA ref="#business.contact-info.telecom.telephone.number">22 21
00</DATA>
   </DATA-GROUP>
  </ENTITY>
  <ACCESS><nonident/></ACCESS> <!-- No login mechanism at this site -->
  <DISPUTES-GROUP>
   <DISPUTES resolution-type="service"
service="http://www.comhem.se/com/telia/ics/portal/apps/startpage/Frame-
set.html?murl=%2Fcom%2Ftelia%2Fics%2Fportal%2Fapps%2Fsupport%2FSupport-
Startpage.html%3Fzid%3D254269261"
     short-description="Bredbandskundtj?nst">
    <REMEDIES><correct/></REMEDIES>
   </DISPUTES>
  </DISPUTES-GROUP>

  <!--Web server logfiles-->
  <STATEMENT>
   <PURPOSE><admin/></PURPOSE>
   <RECIPIENT><ours/></RECIPIENT>
   <RETENTION><stated-purpose/></RETENTION>
   <DATA-GROUP>
    <DATA ref="#dynamic.http"/>
   </DATA-GROUP>
  </STATEMENT>
</POLICY>
</POLICIES>
```

The P3P Files of the Login Domain

It is necessary to create a separate reference file for each domain. Because the site is created in such a way that the domains are separate for the open area and the login area, an identical reference file is used.

https://zone.tewss.telia.se/w3c/p3p.xml

```
<META xmlns="http://www.w3.org/2002/01/P3Pv1">
 <POLICY-REFERENCES>
  <EXPIRY max-age="86400"/>
    <POLICY-REF about="/w3c/policy.xml">
      <INCLUDE>/*</INCLUDE>
    </POLICY-REF>
</POLICY-REFERENCES>
</META>
```

The policy file is again located in the w3c directory.

https://zone.tewss.telia.se/w3c/policy.xml

As you can see, the same human-readable policy and preferences files as at the Comhem site are used.

This file, however, contains a number of statements.

The first one relates to the security logging process and the second to the session cookies. The third contains information about the practices of all the user data that the user provides in forms at the site.

The fourth contains the financial practices. There are no elements in the data schema that could be reused here, so we use the categories instead.

```
<POLICIES xmlns="http://www.w3.org/2002/01/P3Pv1">
 <POLICY name="default"
     discuri="http://www.comhem.se/privacy/policy.html"
     opturi="http://www.comhem.se/privacy/preferences.html"
     xml:lang="en">
  <ENTITY>
   <DATA-GROUP>
    <DATA ref="#business.name">Telia Internet Services</DATA>
    <DATA ref="#business.contact-info.postal.street">Box 7817</DATA><
    <DATA ref="#business.contact-info.postal.postalcode">103 96</DATA>
    <DATA ref="#business.contact-info.postal.city">Stockholm</DATA>
    <DATA ref="#business.contact-info.postal.country">Sweden</DATA>
    <DATA ref="#business.contact-info.online.email">telia-comhem-redak-
tionen@telia.se</DATA>
    <DATA ref="#business.contact-
info.telecom.telephone.intcode">46</DATA>
    <DATA ref="#business.contact-
info.telecom.telephone.loccode">20</DATA>
    <DATA ref="#business.contact-info.telecom.telephone.number">22 21
00</DATA>
   </DATA-GROUP>
  </ENTITY>
```

```
<ACCESS><all/></ACCESS> <!-- Access is given to all data -->
<DISPUTES-GROUP>
 <DISPUTES resolution-type="service"
service="https://zone.tewss.telia.se/com/telia/ics/portal/apps/start-
page/Frameset.html?murl=%2Fcom%2Ftelia%2Fics%2Fportal%2Fapps%2Fsup-
port%2FSupportStartpage.html%3Fzid%3D254269261"
   short-description="Bredbandskundtj?nst">
  <REMEDIES><correct/></REMEDIES>
 </DISPUTES>
</DISPUTES-GROUP>

<!--Web server logfiles-->
<STATEMENT>
 <PURPOSE><admin/></PURPOSE>
 <RECIPIENT><ours/></RECIPIENT>
 <RETENTION><stated-purpose/></RETENTION>
 <DATA-GROUP>
  <DATA ref="#dynamic.http"/>
 </DATA-GROUP>
</STATEMENT>

<!--A session cookie is set-->
<STATEMENT>
 <PURPOSE><current/></PURPOSE>
 <RECIPIENT><ours/></RECIPIENT>
 <RETENTION><no-retention/></RETENTION>
 <DATA-GROUP>
  <DATA ref="#dynamic.cookies"/>
 </DATA-GROUP>
</STATEMENT>

<!--User data-->
<STATEMENT>
 <PURPOSE><current/><admin/><develop/></PURPOSE>
 <RECIPIENT><ours/></RECIPIENT>
 <RETENTION><business-practices/></RETENTION>
 <DATA-GROUP>
  <DATA ref="#user.login.id"/>
  <DATA ref="#user.login.password"/>
  <DATA ref="#user.login.id"/>
  <DATA ref="#user.bdate"/>
  <DATA ref="#user.personname.given"/>
  <DATA ref="#user.personname.family"/>
  <DATA ref="#user.personname.given"/>
  <DATA ref="#user.personname.given"/>
  <DATA ref="#user.home-info.telecom.telephone"/>
  <DATA ref="#user.home-info.telecom.fax"/>
  <DATA ref="#user.home-info.telecom.mobile"/>
 </DATA-GROUP>
</STATEMENT>
```

```
  <!--Payment information-->
  <STATEMENT>
   <PURPOSE><current/></PURPOSE>
   <RECIPIENT><ours/></RECIPIENT>
   <RETENTION><business-practices/></RETENTION>
   <DATA-GROUP>
    <DATA ref="#dynamic.miscdata">
     <CATEGORIES>
      <purchase/>
      <financial/>
     </CATEGORIES>
    </DATA>
   </DATA-GROUP>
  </STATEMENT>
</POLICY>
</POLICIES>
```

The Compact Policy

We translated the policy into a compact policy that is set with the cookies that the site uses. Because these are mostly first-party cookies, the policies are strictly not so necessary to get through the cookie filtering tools described in Chapter 10. Some users may have higher levels of privacy in their settings, and it does not really hurt to have them there.

Because one cookie is set from a different domain—it is third-party technically but first-party legally—the policy was really needed.

The Corresponding Compact Policy

Here it is:

```
P3P: ALL DSP COR CUR ADM DEV OUR BUS UNI PHY ONL PUR FIN COM NAV
```

Acknowledgment

We would like to thank Telia for allowing us to use this information in this book, and we hope that this is a useful example to anyone implementing P3P.

Please do not copy the policies directly—the purpose of this book is to make sure that the special privacy practices of your specific site are described.

APPENDIX D

Positional Privacy Using P3P and LIF Formats

The location of an individual or a mobile terminal can be sensitive information with regard to the privacy of an individual. Giving the individual self-determination for the way position information is used will be crucial to acceptance of the technology. This appendix suggests a solution to how location data can be conveyed in a privacy-friendly way using P3P combined with the PiMI method, as described in Chapter 11.

Location-Based Services

Location, the position of a user (or, rather, the terminal of a user), can be determined in several ways (for an introduction, see [Hjelm 2002]). In brief, the location determination is dependent on sensing the position of a piece of equipment, which can be either dedicated (as in GPS) or a general communications terminal (such as a mobile phone). Having sensed the location of the user and related it either to the network or a global reference system (the methods used in mobile-phone–based network positioning and GPS), it can be expressed in a number of coordinate systems (which are immaterial to this discussion).

In practice, it is very unusual that the user can be positioned to the granularity of his or her terminal (which is often smaller than 10 cm) with any degree of certainty. This is especially true when the user is moving and both the GPS and network-based positioning systems have problems sensing his or her exact position (because not enough satellites can be captured; or because the arc along which the user is moving changes too fast). Indoor location frequently causes problems for positioning systems as well, although less so for network-based positioning. In cases like these, the LIF standard enables the definition of an uncertainty area, which can be used to define the location of the user. In the ideal case, the user can be said to be in the area 10 by 10 cm with an accuracy of 100 percent; however, the lower the accuracy, the larger the area and the smaller the probability. Weighing these, the location determination system can define an area within which the user is with some degree of certainty—for example, a circle with a 100 m radius around the point of the user's assumed position with a certainty of 80 percent.

To be usable in an information service context, the position has to be communicated to the point where information is filtered or assembled (often from a number of different sources). This can be done in the mobile terminal (GPS terminals often have a map database built in), but this requires that the data set be static (as in GPS terminals) or that the data set communicated is small (due to the limited bandwidth available to transmit information to most mobile equipment). In practice, the filtering and assembly of information is done in a server in the network, which also can be the same server that handles all or some of the databases to be used in the creation of the information service.

Location-dependent information services constitute a special case of context-dependent services, where a set of parameters relating to the user's situation is used in creating a specially adapted piece of information that relates to the specific user in that specific situation. One example is services that create a map, which relates the user's current situation to the user's desired situation, according to some set of rules; such as "WHEN 'I am on vacation' AND 'the sun is shining' ARE 'true', THEN 'show me the way to the beach.'" For an introduction and further information about location-dependent services creation and maintenance, see [Hjelm 2002].

The creation of this type of services requires that the position of the terminal be communicated to the server for it to be usable as a parameter in the filtering or construction of information. This is where the privacy risk occurs. If all possible information is communicated to the terminal, and all filtering and assembly are done there, what happens to the information is opaque to the entity maintaining the service. This is impractical in reality, as mentioned. If registered, the position of the user (especially if identifiable and registered over time) in combination with the service (implicitly) requested will enable profiling of the user and thus increase the risk for privacy violations.

The information set describing the user's position has been standardized by the Location Interoperability Forum. The information is defined as an XML document, and the assumption is that the actual information set will be handled at the application layer of the OSI stack, like the information constituting the service. An intermediary, the Mobile Positioning Center, is required to take the data describing the user's position in the network or GPS receiver and put it into a format that is usable by applications (for example, database management systems).

The GEOPRIV Working Group

If information is assembled from many different sources, and if the user can be identified as the same unique user, a very detailed demographic profile can be created over time, which implies that there is a risk of significant privacy violations. One of the favorite use cases of the location information industry is positioned push advertising, where advertisements would be pushed to your mobile phone when you walk past a storefront.

The risk of privacy violation has been of concern to the location information industry for some time (and location information is singled out in recent EU privacy legislation [PETER]). It has also been the focus for work in the Location Interoperability Forum, as well as the GEOPRIV working group in the IETF.

Originally founded to create a generic positioning mechanism for the network layer, the IETF GEOPRIV working group has changed its charter to focus on the privacy issues. Still assuming that an (as yet undefined) object containing the position information will be communicated (through some undefined means) to the server creating the service, the working group has created a requirements document, which takes some initial steps toward describing the mechanisms. The problem defined as the work item is easier to handle in the application layer, using the LIF and P3P protocols, instead of at the network layer.

In addition, the group has discussed some alternate methods to mask the user's position—for example, by generating a number of spurious positions from which a request could have occurred, only one of them being the user's actual position. This "privacy by obscurity" in position-dependent systems is a fallacy, and based on the premise that the user is only ever going to make a request to the information provider, and only that user ever will make that request.

In a system where the user hides his or her position by generating a number of spurious addresses to hide the real position, providing a set of addresses to the service, saying "I am at one of these." Because, however, the probability that the user is in one location (for example, on a street corner) is higher than another (for example, in the middle of a lake), this probability can be used to deduce where the user is, especially because it is likely that all users making requests for information pertaining to a location (for example, directions) will be making requests from a limited set of positions. The actual positions of the users making the request will then form a pattern, whereas the spurious positions will be distributed at random. This means that if there is a desire to violate the user's privacy by knowing his or her position, that can easily be determined.

Setting Up Policies around Location

A statement about privacy practices for location data can be made in two ways. One is by very generally stating that location data is used and needed by the Web site, by using the `<location/>` attribute, as in the example that follows:

```
<STATEMENT>
 <PURPOSE><current/></PURPOSE>
 <RECIPIENT><ours/></RECIPIENT>
 <RETENTION><stated-purpose/></RETENTION>
 <DATA-GROUP>
  <DATA ref="#dynamic.miscdata" optional="no">
   <CATEGORIES>
    <location/>
   </CATEGORIES>
  </DATA>
 </DATA-GROUP>
</STATEMENT>
```

The other option is to use a specific schema. We suggest that the LIF structure be used as a basis for such a schema. This is not necessary if the policy is not being used for data retrieval or if the location in X and Y coordinates is the only thing needed.

In cases where other attributes are needed by the application, a statement like the following can be used.

```
<STATEMENT>
 <PURPOSE><current/></PURPOSE>
 <RECIPIENT><ours/></RECIPIENT>
 <RETENTION><stated-purpose/></RETENTION>
 <DATA-GROUP>
  <DATA
ref="#uaprof.NetworkCharacteristics.SupportedBluetoothVersion"><DATA>
  <DATA ref="#uaprof.BrowserUA.BrowserName"></DATA>
 </DATA-GROUP>
</STATEMENT>
```

User-Agent Response

If the privacy statements of the origin server correspond to the preferences of the user, the user-agent will respond with an LIF-structure containing either a simple X and Y coordinate structure or the elements requested through the suggested data schema.

The simple response expressing only the coordinates of the user would look like the following (the "msid" is the identifier of the terminal, in this case the telephone number; this can be replaced by any identifier):

```
<slia ver="3.0.0" >
    <pos>
    <msid="461011334411">
              <pd>
                     <coord>
                            <X>301628.312</X>
                            <Y>451533.431</Y>
                     </coord>
              <pd>
     </pos>
</slia>
```

This is hardly meaningful, however, because it cannot be assumed that the user is at this specific location, but somewhere near it. Also, there is no time parameter, thus making it impossible to know if this was a recent position or if it relates to the user's position as of a week ago. If more accuracy is required, an area has to be declared for the position and a time to enable freshness. Assuming the user has made the declaration that he or she will give out the time and shape, as in the previous example, and the server has declared that it will not misuse it, the user's response will include the shape and time, as follows (this is actually the normal declaration):

```
<slia ver="3.0.0" >
    <pos>
    <msid="461011334411">
            <pd>
                    <time utc_off="+0200">20020623134453</time>
                    <shape>
                            <CircularArea srsName="www.epsg.org#4004">
                                    <coord>
                                            <X>301628.312</X>
                                            <Y>451533.431</Y>
                                    </coord>
                            <radius>240</radius>
                    </shape>
            <pd>
      </pos>
</slia>
```


About the Method

It is obvious that the method does not offer a complete solution to the problem with user trust in location-based services. There need to be more mechanisms in place—such as a method for guaranteeing that the service provider is trustworthy.

One common way of determining this is that a party the user trusts has authorized the content provider, such as, for example, the ISP or the telecom operator. Another way is through the fact that the service provider is located in a country with strong data protection legislation, meaning that it will be a criminal act not to adhere to the policy. A third way is by letting the user decide the first time the application is used whether it should be trusted in the future, and under which circumstances—for example, assuming the privacy policy is not downgraded.

When used with caution, this method is a very good way of achieving data conveyance while adhering to the user's privacy preferences, and it is far more flexible than any other suggested method.

Additional Reading

Hjelm, Johan. *Creating Location Services for the Wireless Web.* New York: John Wiley & Sons, 2002.

R